RAW. VEGAN. NOT GROSS.

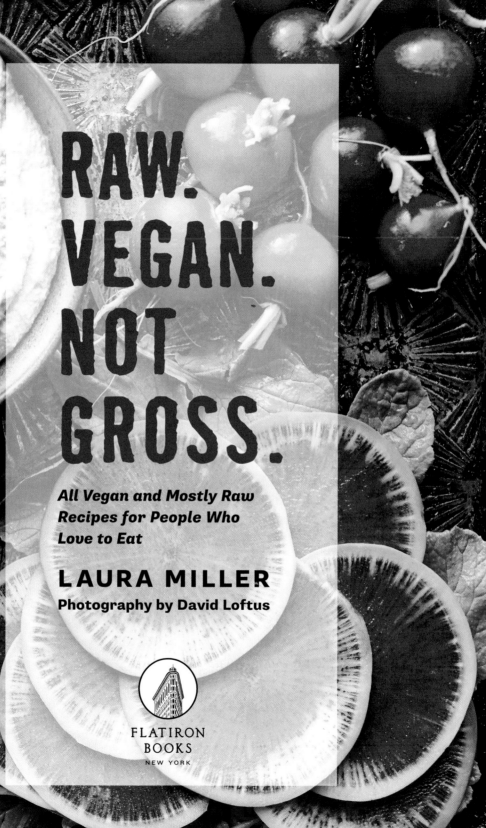

RAW. VEGAN. NOT GROSS.

All Vegan and Mostly Raw Recipes for People Who Love to Eat

LAURA MILLER

Photography by David Loftus

FLATIRON
BOOKS
NEW YORK

FOR MY PARENTS, **BOB AND MAUREEN MILLER.** THANK YOU FOR LOVING ME SO FIERCELY. I AM SO GRATEFUL TO HAVE YOU.

CONTENTS

INTRODUCTION

What I love about raw food is the juiciness and pleasure it adds to everyday life. Eating a mango on your lunch break, scooping the meat out of a coconut in your kitchen, breaking open a pomegranate and watching the seeds burst out—each of these experiences is grounding and connects you to nature in a tangible way. Sure, raw food is credited with glowing skin, bright eyes, shiny hair, and weight loss. But I think eating raw food is really about falling back in love with produce.

I am not fully raw. I'm madly in love with raw food, but I don't have the time, money, or energy to eat raw all the time. It can be incredibly laborious and isolating to try to plan out every single meal in advance because you know you won't be able to find anything you "can eat" at work, while traveling, or at a restaurant. Eating cheeseburgers for every meal isn't healthy, but you know what's also unhealthy? Being constantly stressed about your diet!

Our health is an accumulation of what we put into our bodies. I'd rather go for five years eating mostly plants than try to spend one month eating 100 percent raw only to get frustrated, throw up my hands, and eat cheese puffs for the next four years. It is much more realistic and sustainable to incorporate these kinds of changes into your diet one by one to see which ones work for you. Then you won't have to worry about being the cliché "Oh, yeah, I was raw vegan . . . for a month" guy.

The danger of starting many new "diets" or "lifestyles" is that they often encourage people to abandon their former selves in favor of a newer, shinier version. I am always suspicious of people who flaunt their "after" pictures and talk badly about their previous selves. Wait, that version was you too! And that version of you was the one smart enough and strong enough to realize that you could be happier and healthier. That version of you is the real hero in this story.

We have no shortage of advice and information on how to lose the pounds, get rock-hard abs, and shape the kind of butt you can bounce a quarter off. And sure, all those things are great shiny pennies! But the real change happens when you find a way of taking care of yourself that makes you feel good inside and out, a way that allows you to eat intuitively to nourish your body and mind. It's not about discipline, it's about feeling good. And if it doesn't feel good, it's not going to last.

You want foods that make you feel good now, but that also keep you feeling good five minutes, two hours, and twenty-four hours after you've eaten them. Simply paying attention to how your body feels after you eat something will teach you more than anything I can tell you, and will also lay out a pretty clear roadmap for what you should and shouldn't be eating on a regular basis.

My hope is that more people will come to realize that plant-based diets don't have to be depressing, dogmatic, or cultlike. I see much more benefit for our collective health and environment if most of us eat a plant-based diet than if a handful of us are extreme hard-core raw vegans.

How to use this book

The whole "raw vegan" thing can really scare people off, and I get it: You're already cutting out animal products with veganism, so adding in the raw component, meaning nothing processed or cooked, can feel really restrictive. I personally hate rules when it comes to food, but the boundaries of raw veganism have always felt like a creative challenge for me, and have pushed me to look at produce with fresh eyes. As for me, I eat all vegan and mostly raw. As you'll see in the recipes in this book, that doesn't mean all salads and green smoothies!

You are holding in your hands over a hundred of my favorite recipes from ten years of making and eating raw food. I've organized them by meal, course, and also context: For me, raw food is fun and social and great for parties, which is why I've included an entire chapter on Party Food. If you're just beginning to dip your toes into eating raw, or wanting to share your love of raw food with friends, try pulling some treats from chapters like Sweets or Die Alone (my answer to comfort food, acknowledging the fact that we all want to eat our feelings now and then). Rather than focusing on eliminating foods from your diet, try adding one recipe from Weeknight Dinners into your repertoire each week, or start your mornings with a raw vegan Breakfast. If you're in a hurry, head over to the To-Go chapter for instant meals that will satisfy you while you're checking items off your to-do list.

Of course, if you're already eating mostly (or entirely) raw and vegan, you'll be familiar with the basics and ready to dive into some of the more unusual ingredients and flavor combinations throughout the book. And you'll also find my versions of some raw vegan classics. But, hey, I love my banana soft serve better than any other banana soft serve I've tried, and I sure hope you will too.

No matter where you are in your raw food journey, you'll find that many of the recipes in this book are truly simple, and I've made sure to leave out any ingredients or equipment you can do without. Eating raw doesn't need to be expensive or time consuming. If you're not sure where to start, close your eyes and pick a page at random. You don't need to wait until you're more prepared, or own a fancier blender, or can differentiate among different types of sea vegetables at a casual glance. I hope these recipes will be as fun for you to make as they are for me.

Where this weirdo came from

I grew up with my parents and my older sisters, Mechele and Katie, on a twenty-acre parcel of land in northern California. There were rolling hills, giant oaks, a moss-covered creek that overflowed to the main road during heavy rains, a catfish-filled pond, and a garden that was bursting at the seams.

My dad owned a flooring business and worked very long hours but still managed to keep up a giant garden, a greenhouse, and a little orchard. He is one of those intuitive gardeners—he often didn't know what a plant was called, but always knew how to make it grow. I spent a lot of time going to hardware and feed stores with him on the weekends. He had aviaries where he kept different kinds of birds. At one point, he and I even had a little bird business called Lovebirds R Us where we just sold birds to other breeders and made zero money. I learned to balance a checkbook and handle weird bird people—both skills that came in handy for future life endeavors.

I feel very lucky that I grew up surrounded by so much nature. I spent a lot of time climbing oak trees. In the spring we had entire fields covered with lupine and poppies. We had one hill that served as a fruit tree orchard and a pet cemetery. We would bury our pets, along with any other random dead wildlife we found, in between trees that my dad had planted for each of us: Mom's was apricot, Mechele's was apple, Katie's was plum, and mine was pomegranate. I loved that tree. I would sit under it, easily eating ten pomegranates in one sitting, and then return to the house with every bit of me stained red.

I sometimes look at my adult sisters now, and as different as we have become, I remember that we are all from the same unique place. Sometimes the cows grazing on our property would get out at night and my sisters and I, screaming at each other, would have to work in tandem to shoo them back through the gate. I distinctly remember one day when my older sister Katie, then age nine, had to run outside in her Care Bears nightgown and wield a shovel to kill a rattlesnake that had gotten into one of my dad's aviaries while I stood behind her, shrieking in fear. We climbed a lot of barbed wire fences, had very calloused feet, and spent a lot of time outside naked even after the age when it was probably socially acceptable. On a related note, we got a fair amount of poison oak.

My mom had grown up in a big Irish Catholic family in San Francisco. She was way ahead of her time in her understanding of health, nutrition, and exercise. She made dinner for us every night, feeding us things like "barley bake" (which we of course renamed "barfy bake") that she'd made from scratch. She would allow us to have refined sugar only when we were on vacation, and we were rarely

on vacation. The sugar ban backfired, and the Miller girls were on a constant quest to GET SUGAR. We would sneak spoonfuls of powdered sugar when my mom wasn't looking. I went over to my friends' houses and raided their pantries for sugared cereals and cookies. I was "that kid."

My mom introduced me at a very early age to the idea that food affects how your body feels. It was her reasoning for not getting us donuts after church every Sunday. "You'll eat them and then you'll all be whiny grouches afterward!" she'd say. She was right. Once you start paying attention to which foods give you energy and which ones make you groggy and grouchy, you'll be much more drawn to the good stuff.

Let's talk about my butt

When I was little, my sisters would sing the song about the pig in *Charlotte's Web* but would substitute my name, as in "SHE'S Laura, LAU-ra LAU-ra, LAURA the FA-MOUS PIG!" While I was a chubby little kid, I wasn't overweight, so my sisters were just messing with me. Still, the teasing definitely stuck with me.

Once puberty hit, I started becoming more concerned with my changing body and more aware that I wasn't slim and petite like a lot of my friends. I was very athletic, usually playing two sports at a time. I did have an appreciation of what my body could do, but I also waded through a hormonally charged sea of self-consciousness and resentment with regard to my shape.

By the time I was in high school, my basketball team had made up a pet name for my butt. My coach would even frequently make comments about my butt (which I now realize was an incredibly inappropriate and creepy thing for a middle-aged man to be doing!). I developed a very complicated relationship with my body and soon found myself on the verge of an eating disorder. I don't think anyone consciously intended the butt jokes and comments to be critical, but I couldn't help but hear them as such. Our bodies are so personal and intimate. It takes some of our power away when someone else comments on our appearance, no matter what their intentions are.

Although I never crossed the line into a full-fledged eating disorder, many people close to me did. My older sister suffered from a pretty severe eating disorder. In the span of just a few months, she went from being wild and fearless to frail and weak. Trying to support and help her, my parents got all the best books on eating disorders, *and I devoured them*. I wanted to know the psychology of all this and why this was happening to so many girls I loved. You'd think that studying up on this topic would have kept me safe from succumbing to it. On a conscious level, yes, but I was a relatively social, well-adjusted teenager, which almost by definition meant that I also despised my body.

It infuriates me just thinking about how much brain space and energy girls and women expend day and night worrying about what they are eating (or not eating) and what their thighs look like. I've read enough to understand that it's not all about vanity, either: It's about control, pressure, family dynamics, and shame— all things that should not be related to food.

Our brains are so oversaturated with images of perfect bodies on TV (and Instagram) that we are trained to evaluate and harshly judge both ourselves and others. As women, when we are unhappy in our lives, we often look at our bodies as the reason why. It's as if fixing how we look will be the solution to everything, as opposed to understanding that not liking our bodies is just another symptom of some other, potentially bigger problem. That said, the way you eat and how you fuel your body can greatly affect your mood, hormones, and energy levels, which in turn determines your level of happiness and self-esteem. It's a balance, for sure, and it's an ongoing process.

How I became vegan

When she was about twenty years old, my older sister Katie went all hard-core vegan. I actually found it pretty annoying because she talked about veganism ALL THE TIME and ate legitimately gross food (this was over ten years ago, and there were far fewer vegan options then). I was at first not the slightest bit interested in her new diet, but then, bored on a family vacation, I picked up one of her books on veganism. I read the whole thing in a day and immediately became vegan. The emphasis on health, the environment, and animal rights made it a no-brainer for me. Mind you, I wasn't necessarily doing it right. I was so focused on what I couldn't eat that I didn't have much time or space in my eighteen-year-old brain to think about what I did need to eat to feel good and healthy. I was surviving on Cheerios with soy milk.

So, yeah, I was actually doing it all wrong.

By the time I was in college, I was feeling drained and exhausted. I no longer had sports to keep me sane or give me a sense of community. I'd gained weight, I was always sad and tired, and I was uncomfortable in my body. I was already eating a vegan diet, but I was eating a bunch of processed crap that made me feel terrible. Then I found the book *Raw Food, Real World* (Matthew Kenney and Sarma Melngailis, 2005), and it broke my brain open. This book made me realize that eating vegan is all about produce. And if there is one thing I love, it's produce.

It made instant sense to me that the best way to nourish my body and take care of myself is to eat foods that are as close to their raw state as possible. Plus, I realized that I was naturally attracted to the vibrant colors of fresh food. I loved the way this book taught me to approach food. I learned how a plant-based diet nourishes your body, gives you loads of energy, strengthens your immune system, and regulates your digestion. This was so much more appealing to me than the get-skinny-quick books that just made me feel even more frustrated and worse about myself.

I was getting back to my pomegranate-picking roots, diving into plant-based raw food and loving the benefits. I had increased energy, my weight was getting back to normal, and I felt healthier and stronger than I had in a long time. *Raw Food, Real World* talked about nourishing your body in a holistic way. It was about feeling better in every way.

I started throwing raw dinner parties for all my meat-loving friends to test out recipes, and the response was incredible. There is something about a raw food meal that is energizing and fun—each dinner ended up turning into a giant dance party (although, to be fair, that may have had something to do with the tequila). And my friends loved the food! Like, legitimately, honestly loved it!

Reno, baby

I moved to Reno for love. I'd met a mountain man who had grown up traipsing through the Sierra Nevadas, and he introduced me to backpacking and cold lake swimming. I arrived in Reno and went directly to all the nicest restaurants I could find and asked for a line cook job. I got one, working a line three days a week and then subbing for the baker on her two days off. Had I known what an undertaking this would be, I probably wouldn't have taken the job. I don't think

I had ever baked before in my entire life, but all of a sudden I was making all of the bread, pizza dough for the wood-burning oven, and desserts for a 250-seat restaurant. Not to mention that I wanted desperately not to get in anyone's way and for everyone to DEAR GOD PLEASE JUST LIKE ME.

I put my head down and worked. The sous-chef loved me because he knew I was so hell-bent on learning everything. I barely looked up from my station for the first two months, until finally one of the other line cooks came over to tell me that everyone thought I was doing a good job. From then on I loosened up a bit. Working in a kitchen is unlike any other job. You get paid very little, work your ass off, deal with crazy amounts of stress, and are surrounded by a bunch of big personalities. But man, it's super fun. My head chef gave me the nickname "cutlass"—I think as in the sword you pull out when you really need to win a fight? I never really got it, as I'm not much into swords, but I liked it.

Kitchens can be kind of bro-ey, so it was especially funny that I was getting so into raw vegan food while working in one. I was working a grill for eight hours a night. (I burned off the nerve endings on the tips of my fingers learning to judge different degrees of steak doneness by touch.) All the while, I was bringing in all my latest raw food experiments for snacks between rushes.

It just so happened that around this time, Reno was starting to get hip. A crew of lovely progressives opened a little co-op, and after a few trips in I worked up the courage to ask if I could sell some of my raw cookies there. I packaged up little pairs of lavender macaroons and almond butter cookies, handwrote the ingredients on the labels, and starting bringing a batch to the co-op every week. After a few weeks, I found out that my cookies had caused a rift because a couple of shoppers were buying out the entire lot of them before anyone else could get any. I took this as a sign that I was on the right path, and started researching what my next move might be.

The cult

In 2007, there weren't any real "raw food schools" or training programs (or at least none that I knew of that were affordable), so I opted for an apprenticeship at a raw food retreat center in the desert in the Southwest. From the moment I got there, though, I knew it wasn't the right place for me. It wasn't just that all of the interns were crammed into one room to sleep, or that the pipes froze on day two when everyone was "detoxing" from the food. I'll spare you the gory details, but it was twenty-five sick people sharing one bathroom, and it was gross.

This center was all about restrictions, like not eating fruit because it had too much sugar (I would later learn that there is an entire sect of the raw food world that eats *only* fruit, but that's a whole other thing), not eating onions or garlic because they were "too stimulating" (might cause people to fart in the meditation center), and a slew of other limitations.

There was an apprentice there who went by the name Dandelion. I'm pretty sure he had just changed his name on the drive in. I remember a few people sitting around talking about a man who lived on sunlight alone, and they were talking about what a legend he was, like it was this amazing thing to aspire to. UHHHHMMM NO. That guy never has sex. These were not my people. I wanted lush, sexy, juicy, bright, fun food and people—and sometimes I wanted them with a side of tequila.

By this point in my life, I had known enough people with eating disorders that this way of thinking about food raised my hackles. What this place was offering and pushing felt like a glorified eating disorder disguised as a health movement. That was it. I needed out.

On the third day, I went to the guy in charge and told him I'd had a change of heart, then I packed up my truck and drove fourteen hours home, stopping only for gas and grilled cheese sandwiches. I decided that my love affair with raw vegan food was over.

Here's where it gets real

I'd basically just started to realize that the one thing I was passionate about was a total sham. I no longer had a job, my relationship with my mountain man was on the outs, and I had no idea what I wanted to be doing. I moved back home to live with my parents, and it was then, when I finally took a moment to stop charging ahead and just breathe, that I had the Big Meltdown. I'm talking big. I'm talking I-don't-want-to-be-alive-anymore big. I fell apart. It wasn't pretty.

This is the part where I tell you that healthy eating doesn't solve all of life's problems. I mean, sure, if you don't feel right, it makes sense to take all the steps within your control to feel better. That means exercising, eating well, getting enough sleep, and making sure you're surrounding yourself with positive people. But if you are doing all these things and still feel terrible, or if you're suffering too much to even start doing those things, you need some outside help.

I found a psychologist who saved my life, and who introduced me to the idea that I'd been living with a severe anxiety disorder and essentially just white-knuckling it for about fifteen years. She helped me take active steps to get better. I want to emphasize the fact that getting outside help is not a cop-out. It's smart and it's brave, and it's just another step in doing the work to get better. I'd say that it took about three years to get back on my feet, and it was a very challenging and dark time for me. But it was worth it.

During this time, I was probably still eating mostly vegan, but definitely not on purpose. I felt like I'd gone through a breakup with raw food after realizing that the cult was a sham, and it was an ex that I didn't want to put any more energy into. I was still interested in plant-based eating, but not at the expense of holistic well-being. Feeling better is the whole reason I got into raw food. Nutrition and wellness are very personal issues for me. I care *so much* about people having healthier relationships with their bodies and minds.

Sidesaddle Kitchen

A couple of years (and a few random jobs) later, I started selling raw vegan desserts at a "semi-legal" farmers' market in San Francisco. I named my one-woman business Sidesaddle Kitchen because I thought that women riding sidesaddle were tough as nails and the opposite of the hippie cult image I was trying to stay away from. I made a giant sign with the words "RAW. VEGAN. NOT GROSS." because I was usually the only vegan booth in a sea of pork sandwiches, fried chicken, and bacon-filled chocolates. I wanted people to know that I had the palate of someone who hasn't eaten only raw vegan food all my life, as in "I know what 'real' fudge tastes like, guys—and this is still better."

And it was true. Raw food made me excited because it tasted amazing, and also made me feel great after I ate it. I felt good about giving it to people because I knew exactly how nourishing each bite was.

I had tried and failed at so many things at this point in my career that I had gotten very good at bracing myself for things to not work out. I had originally wanted to sell my sweet treats to coffee shops and markets, but there were a few problems. First, I was afraid to charge enough for my products because I was embarrassed that I was selling "yuppie food" that I couldn't afford to buy if I weren't making it myself. I would sell out at farmers' markets and still not be able to pay my rent!

Second, I was more interested in telling people how to make raw food themselves than selling it to them. People would ask me questions at the markets and I would get their e-mails and follow up to give them my recipes, tell them about how I crafted my signs, or send them links to websites they should be following. As it turns out, this is *not* how you run a business! I made wedding cakes, catered parties, and tried a hundred different things, but was never making money. All this is to say that I became very familiar with the feelings of failure and disappointment. I took a lot of rough jobs (which involved cleaning a lot of public restrooms!), but I was still so passionate about raw food that I kept finding ways to do it—having dinner parties, teaching classes, and eventually making recipe videos.

Recipe videos / introverts gone wild

This might not come across, but I am a sensitive anxious introvert who has no business being in front of a camera.

I started doing recipe videos by accident. The farmers' market where I had been selling my desserts had recently been getting some flak for not being totally legal, so it was doing a little good old-fashioned PR, and they wanted to get the profiles of some of the vendors who were making it work and starting homegrown businesses through the market. A local director, Eric Slatkin, contacted me about doing a profile, and he and the market director came to my house and filmed me talking about my business and making a strawberry tart. I was so nervous that I asked if I could take a shot of tequila. I went into the kitchen and glug-glug-glugged it straight from the bottle, not realizing that I was still wearing my wireless mic, and they could hear the whole thing.

I pretty much forgot about the video and went on my way in survival mode. I eventually decided to shut down my little business because I just needed a real job and was tired of crying about money, so I got a job at a letterpress print and design company and enjoyed the benefits of regular work. A year later, Eric told me that he'd just started working for a YouTube cooking channel called Tastemade and that they liked my video and wanted me to do some recipes.

I actually don't know if I would have done it had I not needed the money so badly. My dream had been to own a business. I'd wanted to be in the kitchen, head down, working. I had never performed or been on any kind of stage, and I was not comfortable being the center of attention, much less having to see my face and hear my voice on video. Now, here I was trying to figure out what kinds of outfits wouldn't make me look like an Oompa Loompa on camera and memorizing explanations about how to best soak nuts with a crew of ten people waiting for me to stop messing up my lines. It was incredibly challenging for me, but I pushed myself to do it even if it meant I'd collapse into a blubbering mess by the end of the day.

Raw. Vegan. Not Gross. was named after the tagline I'd made up for my business in San Francisco. It seemed like the perfect fit because we wanted to make raw vegan videos that were accessible to everyone, not just people who were already

on board with hippie food. The show quickly gained millions of views, and the best part was that I could connect directly with viewers through the comments, so I could answer questions and start to better understand what recipes and information people were really looking for.

Of course, reading the comments also had a downside! I found myself afraid to say/do/make anything because I was so anxious about the criticism I'd get. People criticized my recipes for being too nut-heavy (they were right, and I worked on that!). They criticized my voice (sorry, haterz: I take after my gorgeous and graceful low-voiced mother and I'm not ashamed of that!). They also criticized my weight, and you probably know that this digs into the deepest crevices of your soul and brings up feelings of shame, hurt, self-loathing—the whole bit. It certainly did for me. But I decided that if I stopped doing this just because YouTube commenters told me my thighs were too big, I was missing an opportunity to offer a new voice. A big-thighed voice.

Buzz

I have a dog named Buzz. He's an Akita–pit bull rescue that I adopted as a fully grown dog from the Oakland SPCA eight years ago. He has the soul of Gandhi and the body of Channing Tatum.

He wakes up every morning pumped to be alive. He tiptoes around babies and toddlers because he understands that they are important and delicate. He's only disliked about three people he's ever met, and his intuition was right: They all turned out to be creeps.

Buzz is the mirror I needed. He reflected things back to me that I didn't expect. For example, Buzz was really stressed when I brought him to certain friends' houses, panting and pacing around and generally just uncomfortable. I finally realized that he was just mirroring my discomfort in those situations. I know this sounds crazy, but I started reading him as a way of understanding myself. I made a point to focus on friendships that made me feel supported and relaxed. I chose a more peaceful living situation rather than one in a hipper part of town. He taught me to stop pushing, to go with the current instead of always swimming upstream, to take better care of myself. I am one of those types who

RAW. VEGAN. NOT GROSS.

always thinks they have to do everything the hard way. But guess what? The hard way wasn't always the right way.

Having a dog has caused me to interact with the world differently. I find myself talking to people more. Dudes on the street who would usually make some misogynistic comment as I walked by would now ask earnestly what kind of dog he is and how old.

I was always one of those rock-solid types who didn't cry at weddings or funerals or really . . . ever. Seeing how much my friends love my dog and how much he loves them has brought us closer. He's like my heart outside of my body. Intuitive, confident, and smart as a whip, he is everything I want to be.

For me, being healthy isn't just about the food. It's about figuring out the things that either lift me up or wear me down. As weird as it sounds, Buzz has helped me to become more cognizant of what and who I need in my life to feel better and be happier.

Look, I'm just doing my best, okay?

And to be honest, I'm still figuring it out. The amount of hustling I've done to make ends meet while trying to promote wellness and healthy body image has sometimes left me drained, and occasionally made me feel like a giant hypocrite. As in, "I only have $10 in my bank account and these cheese puffs are the only gluten-free thing at the corner store and it's probably not real cheese anyway . . . so that's okay, right? Ugh, definitely not gonna Instagram this one!"

Between sublets and breakups and dog-sitting in exchange for a place to sleep, I moved about eight times in three years (San Francisco is insanely expensive and not very dog-friendly!). Dealing with the logistics of making money while also trying to put out interesting content that I believed in put me in a state of constant white-knuckling. I started having really bad back pain, so I went to my neighborhood chiropractor. In one of our sessions, he asked offhand if I felt healthy, and I said, without skipping a beat, OH, HELL NO. This is insane, right? I do videos on raw vegan food! I have an Instagram account that basically just documents my love affair with produce! THIS MAKES NO SENSE!

I was feeling crappy. Like, really crappy. I grabbed a piece of construction paper and scribbled down a pep talk to myself. I read it aloud to myself every morning for the next week or so.

> Laura Miller.
>
> Take care of yourself.
>
> Your body is awesome and special. Take care of it. Nourish it.
> Move it. Not for any reason other than it will feel good
> and help you feel better.
>
> You need to set an example of relaxed strength.
> Strong with ease.
>
> Laura Miller.
>
> Take care of yourself.

Can you imagine me doing this? WAIT STOP PLEASE DON'T, because I definitely looked just as crazy as you're imagining.

But here's the thing: It actually worked. I started drinking more water. I started eating more leafy greens. I made myself exercise even when I felt exhausted and terrible, because that's when I needed it most. My body and I were on the same team.

Maybe it was the act of saying it out loud, as if I were telling a friend to take care of herself (i.e., "not for any other reason other than it will feel good and help you feel better"), but I almost felt like subconsciously I had been taking worse care of myself because I was retaliating against the YouTube commenters who called me too chubby, too manly, too whatever. I felt like exercising would be some sort of admission that I was responding to their tacky insults. But no, I was doing it for my body, as if I was taking care of her. To make her feel better, as I would for a friend. And this way of framing it worked for me, because I don't want my best friend to look skinnier or prettier, I just want her to feel better.

I hope you love this food as much as I do. But more than that, I hope you remember to love your body and take care of it as well as you possibly can.

Laura Miller.
Take care of yourself.
Your body is awesome and special.
Take care of it. Nourish it. Move
it. Not for any reason other than
it will feel good and help you feel
better.
You need to set an example of
relaxed strength. Strong with ease.
Laura Miller. Take care of yourself.

RAW. VEGAN. NOT GROSS.

The basics

People ask me a lot of questions about health, which I often do not feel qualified to answer given that I'm not a doctor, nutritionist, or naturopath. I have, however, been reading, experimenting, and talking to people about health and wellness since I was a teenager. Everyone wants the same things: glowing skin, a happy weight, a digestive system that they don't have to think much about (i.e., no issues in "either direction"), and to stop getting sick so much.

Here are a few of my go-tos for revamping your diet:

Fermented Veggies

My first instinct when someone tells me that they have a digestive or skin issue is to ask if they're eating fermented vegetables and, if not, to tell them to get on that. They are vegetables on steroids. They help regulate your digestion, boost immunity, and even help your body absorb other nutrients so that you can really get the most out of all the foods you're eating. Sauerkraut, kimchi, or whatever you like—just get it in there. I have also noticed that since I've started getting serious about eating fermented veggies every day, my cravings for sweets have really decreased. Not only does the gut-healing beneficial bacteria help to balance a healthier inner ecosystem, but it also helps my body to better handle the sugars and toxins that I'm eating.

Healthy Fats

Please, please, please do not be afraid of fats. There is a significant portion of the raw food community that believes in eating mostly fruit and hardly any fat. I don't think this is smart, and I can say from personal experience that it made me feel like crap. Healthy, plant-based fats feed your brain, prime your body to absorb nutrients, and keep you feeling full both physically and mentally. When in doubt, put some avocado on it.

Dark Leafy Greens

Kale, spinach, chard, arugula, whatever you like—these are some of the most nutrient-dense foods on the planet. They are all packed with iron, vitamins, minerals, antioxidants, and even protein! They help prevent cancer, heart disease, and high cholesterol. As a side note, my dad and I raised birds when I was little, and he would grow a garden full of chard specifically to feed them—even birds need their greens!

Hydration

I have to admit, this one is the hardest for me. I never remember to drink enough water. Most of us are dehydrated all the time, and that sucks, because it makes us tired, hungry, and even anxious. Do whatever you have to do: Stick Post-its to your fridge, get a water drinking app on your phone, or just try to keep your reusable bottle with you and full at all times.

Get Alkaline

Chances are your body is too acidic. Sugar, coffee, alcohol, meat—they all create acidity in the body. This can lead to symptoms like inflammation, a weakened immune system, water retention, skin rashes, sleep issues, mood swings, fatigue, and allergies. The best and easiest way to start getting alkaline is to have warm water with lemon first thing in the morning, every morning.

Equipment guide

If you're just getting started with raw food, don't feel like you have to go out and buy everything all at once. Start with what you've got, then figure out which things you feel like you're missing. The worst thing is to spend a bunch of money on kitchen stuff that will just take up shelf space.

Vitamix / Blendtec / Ninja

"Will this one-speed blender from 1988 that I inherited from my older sister work?" Yes! Well, it will for a while, but then you'll find that it just doesn't cut it and you need to upgrade. On a personal note, I find that listening to a blender trying desperately to blend is just emotionally exhausting and makes me feel equally desperate. Like, all those times I kept texting boys who didn't like me desperate. Invest in a good one if you can, and your raw food game will be significantly improved.

Good Knives

Sharp knives keep you from cutting yourself. Trust me, I cut myself a lot, which you know if you've ever seen my videos. While I have to admit that part of this is that my knife skills are about that of a toddler cutting up Play-Doh, the other part is that for a while we had the dullest, crappiest knives in the studio. Dull knives invite sloppy, put-your-back-into-it technique, which inevitably leads to cuts. Basically, if you decide not to invest in good knives, I encourage you to invest in a cute Caboodle and fill it with cute bandages.

Food Processor

A lot of people wonder why they need a food processor if they already have a blender. A food processor works better for thick doughs or crusts without a lot of moisture which can get stuck in a blender, and is also better for mixing pestos and things that you want to keep a little chunky.

Mandoline

You can get a pretty high-quality plastic mandoline at any kitchen store for about $20. They are great for cutting any fruits or vegetables that need to be uniformly sliced. Be sure to use the safety guard, though!

Spiralizer

I only just got a spiralizer of my own in the last few months, so I can attest to the fact that it's really not a necessity, but it's super handy and fun to make uniform noodles out of vegetables like zucchini. If you're not into having another gadget in your kitchen, you can use your mandoline to get a thin julienne that will work fine too.

Dehydrator

Dehydrating is a way to "cook" raw foods while keeping them at a low temperature so that they are still "raw" and maintain their full nutritional value. I love my dehydrator and use it to make crackers, crusts, kale chips, and basically anything crispy! I love it because I never have to worry about overcooking and can just set it and forget it, waking up the next morning to finished cookies or kale chips. That said, I am hesitant to tell anyone to get a dehydrator, because most people end up using it twice, then shoving it into a closet and forgetting about it. Especially if you're just starting out, an oven kept at a low temp works fine. If you find yourself wanting a dehydrator, go for it. I recommend the kind with square shelves that you can put nonstick sheets on.

Microplane

A tiny little gadget that can add so much! I use it mostly for zesting lemons and grating nutmeg directly into dessert fillings. It pumps the flavor up exponentially.

Sweeteners

This feels like a loaded topic. A lot of raw vegans are "high carb, low fat," meaning that they eat a lot of fruit. While I am a big supporter of fresh fruit, I just can't get on board with that. I tried it for a while and I felt terrible. My blood sugar levels were on a constant roller coaster, as were my mood swings. No thanks (hair toss). For this same reason, I am also not a big proponent of juicing. Unless they are made of just straight greens, juices are usually loaded up with fruit, and without the fiber of actually eating the fruit, it's a straight shot of sugar to your bloodstream.

Stevia

Because stevia is usually seen in a white powdered form, a lot of people have trouble differentiating it from the horrible chemical-laden diet sweeteners that you find on the tables of most diners. Stevia is an herb that is three hundred times sweeter than sugar, so it needs to be used sparingly and in the right context. It can have a slight aftertaste in foods, but works great in drinks. I use stevia in my coffee, in smoothies, and in green shakes. It has *zero* effect on blood sugar, which is incredible for those with diabetes, people trying to lose weight, or those who are just watching their blood sugar levels. It also has zero calories.

Yacón Syrup

Yacón syrup tastes a lot like molasses, but has about half the calories of the same amount of honey or sugar and doesn't cause the giant blood sugar spike of either of them. You can use yacón syrup in any recipe that calls for maple syrup.

Coconut Sugar

Coconut sugar has a flavor and texture reminiscent of brown sugar. It's low-glycemic and does not spike insulin levels, and is also a great source of B-vitamins, zinc, magnesium, potassium, and iron.

Maple Syrup

First things first: Maple syrup isn't raw. It's just as sweet as sugar, but has fewer calories and very high levels of zinc to support your immune system. Make sure to get pure maple syrup, and choose grade B over grade A, as grade B has a high mineral content.

Raw Honey

While it's not vegan, I love using raw honey. Make sure that it's actually raw, though! Unpasteurized and unfiltered honey should be solid and not pourable. It's incredibly nutritious, packed with amino acids, enzymes, and B-vitamins, so I find that I use it more as a supplement than a sweetener in cooking or baking.

Agave Nectar

I'm not a big fan of agave. It has become incredibly popular over the past decade, and lauded as a lovely viscous sweetener with a neutral flavor that's easy to use. I recommend that you use agave very sparingly, as it contains nearly 90 percent fructose, has no nutritional value, and is a highly processed sugar that can have detrimental long-term effects.

The pantry

almond butter

almond milk (unsweetened)

buckwheat groats

chia seeds

cinnamon

coconut flakes (unsweetened)

cocoa powder and/or raw cacao powder

flaxseeds

mustard

nutritional yeast

sauerkraut

sea salt or Himalayan salt

sea vegetables

tamari (gluten-free soy sauce)

vanilla extract

sweeteners:

coconut sugar

maple syrup

raw honey (not vegan)

stevia

yacón syrup

oils:

cold-pressed extra-virgin coconut oil

cold-pressed extra-virgin olive oil

flours:

brown rice flour

gluten-free oat flour

BREAKFASTS

Eating breakfast is important. This is your one opportunity to put some serious nutrition in your body before the day gets crazy. Eating breakfast gets your metabolism going and sets you up to make better food choices throughout the rest of the day. That said, you don't want to just throw any old thing in your body. You need plant-based fat, protein, and nutrients that are going to keep you going strong and that will prevent you from having a sugar crash at 10 A.M.

My sisters and I weren't allowed to eat "sugared cereals" unless we were on vacation or it was a holiday. Otherwise, we weren't permitted to get any cereal in which sugar was listed earlier than the fourth ingredient. So on every shopping trip, you could find all three Miller girls trolling the cereal aisle just praying that at least one frosted cereal would fit the bill. None ever did, but the experience made a lasting impact on all of us about how much ingredients matter and forced us to get creative about feeding a sweet tooth.

BANANA PANCAKES

cooked • 6 pancakes

MY DAD USED TO MAKE my sisters and me
Mickey Mouse pancakes on Saturday mornings.
For the layman, that's one big pancake with two
smaller pancakes attached as ears. They were
topped with chocolate chip eyes, a maraschino
cherry nose, and a whipped cream smile. They
were big fluffy plates of nostalgia in the making.
Ours were usually just made out of Bisquick mix,
so this version would have been a solid upgrade.
These pancakes are packed with fiber, omegas,
protein, and potassium, but beyond that they
have a light sweetness from the banana and
coconut oil, a nuttiness from the oat flour, and
a light and fluffy mouthfeel.

Active time: 15 minutes
Inactive time: 15 minutes

2 ripe bananas

¼ cup ground flaxseeds
soaked in ¾ cup water
for 15 minutes to 1 hour

¼ cup coconut oil, plus
more for cooking

½ cup almond milk

1½ cups gluten-free
oat flour (or other
gluten-free flour)

1 teaspoon baking soda

1 teaspoon cinnamon

Pinch of salt

Optional toppings:
maple syrup, fruit,
coconut whipped
cream (see page 178),
chocolate chips

1. Mash the bananas in a small bowl, then
   add the flaxseed-water mixture, coconut
   oil, and almond milk. Mix well.

2. In another medium bowl, whisk all the dry
   ingredients together.

3. Fold in the wet ingredients, using a spatula
   to mix until well incorporated.

4. Preheat a cast-iron skillet over medium
   heat and coat with coconut oil.

5. Ladle ¼ cup of the batter at a time into your
   medium-hot skillet. After 2 to 3 minutes,
   you'll see bubbles pop and then form
   holes that stay open on the surface of the
   pancake. Slide a thin spatula under each
   pancake and then flip with a quick flick
   of the wrist.

6. Cook for another 1 to 2 minutes, until the
   underside is golden brown. Remove from
   the skillet when fully cooked.

7. Top with maple syrup, fruit, coconut
   whipped cream, or chocolate chips!

AVOCADO GRAPEFRUIT BOWLS

mostly raw • 2 servings

I AM SCARED OF EVERYTHING. Seriously, I panic about having to go to the post office. But you know what I'm not afraid of? Fat. Fat is an important part of your diet, and I can guarantee you that your body is craving it right now. A lot of folks are deathly afraid of eating fats because they think fats "make you fat." This is a myth. Healthy, plant-based fats help to prevent inflammation, allow your body to absorb other nutrients, support healthy brain function, keep you feeling full, and lower cholesterol. The healthy fats in the avocado help your body to absorb vitamin C and potassium, and the basil is a great anti-inflammatory and supports cardiovascular health, making this a great breakfast for athletes.

I eat this straight from the avocado, but you could also scoop it out and spread the whole thing on toast.

Active time: 5 minutes

2 ruby red grapefruits

2 avocados

3 or 4 fresh basil leaves

1 teaspoon maple syrup

Pinch of salt

1. Remove both the peel and pith from the grapefruit using a sharp paring knife. Working over a medium glass bowl to catch the juice, carefully carve out the grapefruit segments from between the membranes. Reserve the juice in the bowl.

2. Transfer the grapefruit segments to a small glass bowl and set aside.

3. Cut the avocados in half, remove each pit, and place the halves in a medium bowl or on a cutting board.

4. Pour the reserved grapefruit juice over the avocados to keep them from browning.

5. Cut your basil into chiffonade by stacking the leaves on top of one another, then rolling into a cigar. Holding the roll against the cutting board, thinly slice it crosswise to create ribbons.

6. Add the basil to the small bowl with the grapefruit segments, maple syrup, and salt. Toss lightly, then scoop the mixture onto the avocado halves, filling in where the pit has been removed. It's okay if it spills over a bit!

7. Serve immediately.

CRÊPES

cooked • 6 to 8 crêpes

I'M JUST NOT A BRUNCH PERSON. The process of going to a restaurant, constantly apologizing to the waitress for being a big group/finicky/alive, and GOD FORBID SPLITTING THE CHECK is just a living nightmare.

Brunch at home is the way to go. Add in the homemade hazelnut chocolate spread if you really want to make your friends love you.

These crêpes aren't super sweet, so you could also fill them with something savory (like sautéed onions and sweet potatoes!) and they'd be a delicious breakfast-for-dinner.

Active time: 30 minutes
Inactive time: 2 hours

2 tablespoons chia seeds soaked in ⅓ cup water for 15 minutes to 1 hour

1 cup brown rice flour

1 cup gluten-free oat flour

1 teaspoon coconut sugar

¼ teaspoon salt

Coconut oil

Optional toppings: sliced fruit, nuts, honey, maple syrup, or Hazelnut Chocolate Spread (recipe follows)

1. Put the chia-water mixture, 2 cups water, the flours, sugar, and salt in a food processor and mix until thoroughly combined.

2. Put the mixture in the refrigerator and chill for at least 2 hours.

3. Heat a 9-inch nonstick frying pan over low heat, adding enough coconut oil to lightly coat the pan.

4. Pour ½ cup of the mixture into the pan at an angle, spreading the batter out by using a circular motion to tilt the pan around. The batter should be the consistency of heavy cream. If it's too thick, add water 1 tablespoon at a time.

5. Cook over medium heat for 1 to 2 minutes, until the crêpe is evenly browned and the edges start to peel away from the sides of the pan.

6. Gently flip in the pan and cook for an additional 1 to 2 minutes.

7. Repeat until all the batter has been used up.

8. Fill with your favorite fruit, nuts, honey, maple syrup, or Hazelnut Chocolate Spread and serve.

continued

HAZELNUT CHOCOLATE SPREAD

mostly raw • about 2 cups

Active time: 10 minutes

1 cup hazelnuts, soaked overnight in 3 to 4 cups water

⅓ cup maple syrup

⅓ cup coconut oil

1 teaspoon vanilla extract

¼ teaspoon sea salt

¼ cup cocoa powder

¼ cup almond milk or water

1. Drain and rinse the hazelnuts. Place in a high-speed blender or food processor. Blend until smooth, smooshing down the sides as needed (this may take up to 10 minutes).

2. Once the hazelnuts turn into a buttery consistency, add the maple syrup, coconut oil, vanilla, salt, and cocoa powder and blend until smooth. Slowly add the almond milk and blend until you arrive at a creamy and buttery consistency.

GINGER MAPLE GRANOLA

mostly raw • 8 to 10 servings

I THINK OF GRANOLA AS one of those things that people order for breakfast at restaurants because they are "trying to be healthy." It seems like a good choice, but conventional granola is usually way too sweet and also contains gluten, which for me is just a recipe for a stomachache.

As much as some people are annoyed with the influx of "gluten-free" marketing and think it's all a big sham, I just can't deny how much better I feel when I don't eat gluten. While only about 1 percent of the population has celiac disease, many others experience everything from inflammation to headaches to bloating after eating gluten.

I wanted this to be an immunity-boosting, beautifying granola. That meant adding lemon and ginger for immunity, buckwheat groats and oats for fiber, cinnamon to help control blood sugar, and coconut oil and chia seeds to boost metabolism and make my skin glow. It just so happened that this combination of flavors was dynamite. You can eat it with almond milk or just keep a zip-top bag of it nearby for snacking.

Active time: 30 minutes
Inactive time: 30 minutes or 12 hours

2 cups buckwheat groats soaked in water for at least 1 hour or up to overnight

1 cup gluten-free oats

1 cup coconut flakes (or pumpkin seeds if you prefer)

¼ cup chia seeds

1 teaspoon grated fresh ginger, or ½ teaspoon ground ginger

¼ cup coconut oil

½ cup maple syrup

1 teaspoon vanilla extract

2 teaspoons cinnamon

Grated zest and juice of 1 lemon

1 teaspoon salt

Pinch of stevia

1. Drain and rinse the groats, drain again, and then place them in a large glass bowl.

2. Add the oats, coconut flakes, and chia seeds and mix.

3. Combine all the remaining ingredients in separate bowl and mix.

4. Fold the wet mixture into the dry mixture.

5. Spread on a teflex sheet and dehydrate overnight, or spread on a parchment-lined baking sheet and bake in the oven at 350°F for 30 minutes, pulling it out halfway through to flip it and break it into small bite-sized chunks. Store in an airtight container for up to a week.

FEEL BETTER GREEN SHAKE

raw • 1 shake

IF YOU NEED YOUR GREEN SHAKE to taste like a piña colada in order to stomach it, turn the page; this isn't for you! This is the advanced green smoothie. It's alkalinizing, low-glycemic, and packed with vitamins and antioxidants to keep your energy up, your skin glowing, and your immune system charged. That said, you can make this nutritional powerhouse more accessible and tasty by replacing the kale with a sweeter leafy green like spinach, or adding some frozen banana to up the sweetness and creaminess.

Active time: 5 minutes

1½ cups water or almond milk

1 grapefruit, peeled

Pinch of stevia

Pinch of cinnamon

1 tablespoon grated fresh ginger

1 bunch kale (or spinach), washed and chopped

1 cup chopped green apple

½ cucumber

1 cup ice, or 1 frozen banana, halved

1. In a high-speed blender, blend the water and grapefruit.

2. Add the stevia, cinnamon, and ginger and pulse a couple of times.

3. Add the kale one handful at a time, blending, then adding more and blending again until it has all been incorporated.

4. Add the apple, cucumber, and ice and blend until smooth.

5. Add additional ice if needed.

APPLE CINNAMON PARFAIT

mostly raw • 4 or 5 servings

IF YOU'RE THE TYPE WHO wakes up in the morning already thinking about dessert, this one's for you. It's the next best thing to having an ice cream sundae for breakfast.

There are three parts to this parfait. Each is delicious and should be considered secret weapons in a plant-based breakfast (or dessert!) arsenal. Fix it all up in a little glass jar, and you've got a sweet little parfait that will impress even the most discerning dairy lover.

Active time: 30 minutes
Inactive time: 1 hour or 12 hours

For the cashew cream:
2 cups raw cashews

½ cup maple syrup

¼ cup fresh lemon juice

1 teaspoon vanilla extract

½ cup coconut oil

Pinch of salt

For the baked apples:
2 apples

1 tablespoon coconut oil

1 teaspoon vanilla extract

1 teaspoon cinnamon

Pinch of salt

For the buckwheat crunchies:

2 cups buckwheat groats soaked in water for at least 1 hour

½ cup maple syrup

2 teaspoons cinnamon

1 teaspoon salt

⅛ teaspoon stevia

1. Make the cashew cream: Soak the cashews in water for at least 1 hour, then drain and put in a food processor.

2. Add the maple syrup, lemon juice, vanilla, coconut oil, and salt, then blend until the cream is completely smooth.

3. Make the baked apples: Core and thinly slice the apples and toss them with the coconut oil, vanilla, cinnamon, and salt.

4. Spread on a teflex sheet and dehydrate overnight, or bake on a Silpat sheet in the oven at 200°F for 1 hour.

5. Make the buckwheat crunchies: Drain and rinse the groats, drain again, and then place them in a medium bowl.

6. Add all the remaining ingredients to the bowl and mix thoroughly.

7. Spread on a teflex sheet and dehydrate overnight, or bake on a Silpat sheet in the oven at 200°F for 1 hour.

8. Place the apples, crunchies, and cashew cream in a bowl, alternating layers, and serve.

COCOA BUCKWHEAT CRISPIES

mostly raw • 10 servings

I'VE BEEN A BIG FAN OF buckwheat groats ever since I started getting into raw food. As someone who was experiencing sticker shock at a lot of the other raw food ingredients, groats were my salvation. They are really cheap, especially if you can find them in the bulk section. Groats are actually seeds that, when soaked and dehydrated or baked, become crispy, airy, and a little bit nutty. They also have a crunch that is incredibly satisfying in granolas and cereals.

Active time: 5 minutes
Inactive time: 1 hour or 12 hours

2 cups buckwheat groats, soaked in water for at least 1 hour or up to overnight

½ cup maple syrup

½ cup cocoa powder

1 teaspoon salt

Pinch of stevia

Pinch of cinnamon

Almond milk

1. Drain and rinse the groats, drain again, and then place them in a medium bowl.

2. Add the maple syrup, cocoa powder, salt, stevia, and cinnamon to the bowl and mix thoroughly.

3. Spread the mixture on a teflex sheet and dehydrate overnight, or bake on a Silpat sheet in the oven at 200°F for 1 hour, breaking them into smaller pieces if they are drying in chunks.

4. Remove from the dehydrator or oven and let cool.

5. Pour almond milk over a bowl of crispies. Cereal. Done.

BREAKFAST ROLL-UP

raw • 1 roll-up

THIS IS ONE OF THOSE MIRACLES of the raw food world. It shouldn't taste good (I mean, you're eating a raw chard leaf for breakfast? WTF?), but it's some kind of delicious vegan voodoo. The combination of the sweetness of the banana with the earthiness of the chard, and the sweet creaminess of the almond butter—it's just magic. It only takes two minutes, and it just might change your whole life. Like, turn you into one of those people who meditates every morning and never curses and prays for people who cut in front of them in line. TRY IT.

Active time: 5 minutes

1 rainbow chard leaf

2 tablespoons almond butter

1 banana, cut into pieces

1. Flip the leaf over so that the side with the prominent spine is facing up. Using a paring knife, carefully start to shave off the spine, starting near the bottom, where it begins to protrude most, carving the vein down a bit.

2. Spread the almond butter in the middle of the leaf. Set the banana pieces on top of the leaf.

3. Roll the leaf around the banana and almond butter. Eat.

RAW. VEGAN. NOT GROSS.

ALKALINIZING MORNING CLEANSER

raw • 1 serving

TRYING TO DO A TOTAL health overhaul can be super overwhelming, and then ultimately discouraging when everything doesn't go perfectly. Lemon water in the morning is one of the easiest habits to get into, and also packs a giant nutritional punch. It's alkalinizing to the body, boosts your immunity with vitamin C and potassium, aids digestion, and helps keep your skin clear and glowing.

Active time: 5 minutes

1 cup warm water

Juice of ½ lemon

Extra credit add-ins:

¼ teaspoon ground cayenne (metabolism booster, decongestant, pain reliever)

1 tablespoon grated fresh ginger (circulation improver, stomach soother)

1 tablespoon grated fresh turmeric (powerful anti-inflammatory)

½ teaspoon raw honey (antimicrobial, antiviral, and antifungal)

1. Put the warm water in your favorite mug, then squeeze in your lemon juice.

2. Sprinkle in one or more extra-credit supplements, if desired, and stir.

3. Drink first thing in the morning (every morning!).

TURMERIC TONIC

raw • 2 servings

I THINK THAT TURMERIC ROOT is the second coming. It's powerful stuff that's got anti-inflammatory properties and a bangin' color to boot. It's really the most beneficial when taken in raw form, but it's a little tricky to know how to do that if you're not into just shooting it straight (which I pretend I like but is actually pretty gross).

I combine the turmeric juice with persimmon, which is one of my favorite fall fruits with an almost identical sunny hue, and cut the whole thing with some acidity from lemon. The result is a juice that tastes as bright and sunny as it looks.

Active time: 5 minutes

2 persimmons

2 lemons, peeled

1 (3-inch) piece fresh turmeric root

1. Process all the ingredients through a juicer, and add water as needed.

2. Enjoy immediately for optimal benefits!

RAW. VEGAN. NOT GROSS.

BLACKBERRY CHIA MUFFINS

cooked • 12 muffins

I WAS ALWAYS THE KID TO lick the frosting off and then offer the rest of my cupcake to some other chocolate-faced chump, so it kind of goes without saying that I never understood the appeal of muffins. Even as an adult, after my frosting addiction had subsided, whenever someone would bring a clamshell six-pack of pure white muffins, each the size of a small dog, I still didn't get it. It's like eating dry air but with lots of empty calories, so you're starving ten minutes after you eat it.

I decided that if I were going to go over to the dark side and get into muffins, I was gonna do it my way: no crappy white flours or refined sugars or fluff. I experimented and made a ton of very gross batches until finally creating the recipe here. These muffins are dense and moist, but also packed with fiber and protein to keep you fueled. I've used blackberries in this version, but you could really use whatever fruit is in season.

Active time: 30 minutes
Inactive time: 45 minutes

1¼ cups almond flour

1 cup gluten-free oat flour

½ cup coconut sugar

2 teaspoons baking powder

1 teaspoon baking soda

½ teaspoon salt

3 tablespoons chia seeds, soaked in ½ cup water for 15 minutes to 1 hour

1 cup applesauce

⅓ cup coconut oil

1 tablespoon vanilla extract

2 cups blackberries

1. Preheat the oven to 350°F. Line a muffin pan with liners.

2. In a large bowl, stir together the flours, coconut sugar, baking powder, baking soda, and salt.

3. In another bowl, combine the chia-water mixture, applesauce, coconut oil, almond milk, and vanilla. Whisk by hand until smooth.

4. Add to the flour mixture and blend just until moistened but still lumpy. Fold in the blackberries.

5. Spoon the batter into 12 muffin cups, filling each cup about two-thirds full. Bake until springy to the touch, 25 to 30 minutes.

6. Let cool for 5 minutes, then transfer the muffins to a wire rack to cool completely.

DONUTS

cooked • 12 donuts

WITH THEIR CRISPY EDGES and fluffy sweet centers, and covered in a glistening chocolate glaze, these donuts are pure heaven. I've used almond and sorghum flours because they are full of protein, healthy fats, and fiber. That means your body can actually recognize them as human food and not freak out, leaving you crying in a ball on the floor in an hour.

Active time: 30 minutes
Inactive time: 20 minutes

1 cup almond flour

1 cup sorghum flour

1 cup potato starch

1½ teaspoons baking powder

½ teaspoon baking soda

¼ teaspoon xanthan gum

½ teaspoon salt

¾ cup maple syrup

⅓ cup Applesauce (recipe follows)

½ cup hot water

⅓ cup coconut oil

Juice of 1 lemon

Chocolate Glaze (recipe follows)

1. Preheat the oven to 325°F.

2. Mix the dry ingredients in a large glass bowl.

3. Mix the wet ingredients in another large glass bowl.

4. Add the wet ingredients to the dry ones, and mix with a spatula until thoroughly combined.

5. Using a spoon, put ¼ cup batter into each donut mold and make sure it's spread all the way around.

6. Bake for 10 minutes, rotate, then bake for another 5 to 7 minutes, until browned on the top and cooked through.

7. If you'd like, dip the top half of each donut into chocolate glaze.

APPLESAUCE

cooked • 3 cups

You can, of course, just use unsweetened store-bought applesauce. But if you have the time, homemade applesauce will make your donuts taste extra fresh.

Active time: 15 minutes
Inactive time: 40 minutes

1½ pounds apples

2 teaspoons cinnamon

¼ cup maple syrup

3 tablespoons fresh lemon juice

1. Preheat the oven to 325°F. Line a baking sheet with parchment paper.

2. Peel, core, and chop the apples into 1-inch chunks.

3. Toss the apples with the cinnamon, maple syrup, and lemon juice.

4. Spread the apples over the prepared baking sheet and bake for 40 minutes, rotating halfway through.

5. Let cool completely, then transfer to a food processor and puree.

CHOCOLATE GLAZE

mostly raw • 1½ cups

Dipping donuts in this glaze is super-duper fun.

Active time: 5 minutes

1 cup coconut oil

¾ cup cocoa powder

2 tablespoons maple syrup

Pinch of salt

Blend all the ingredients until smooth, then place in a shallow bowl for donut dipping!

TO GO

When I was growing up, my dad had a flooring business—tile, carpet, hardwood, that kind of thing. My two older sisters both worked in his office during their summer breaks, but because of my tomboy style and general ability to bro down, I got to go into the field to do repairs and stuff with my dad's right-hand man, Jerry. If I'm being honest, this was probably the most cush job I've ever had, because it was mostly just riding around in Jerry's truck with him in between doing repairs at construction sites.

Jerry—then in his late thirties—is a jolly, rosy-cheeked man who has never in his life driven anything other than a truck. He is a total ham and loves to throw around off-color jokes to get a rise out of me, but he is kind and smart and has been through enough in his life that he knows that none of the little stuff matters. He is also diabetic, so he always had a black leather fanny pack in his truck.

Jerry eats like a ten-year-old boy without adult supervision. We would stop at a gas station on our way out in the early-morning hours, and he'd go inside to get a Big Gulp, beef jerky, and some Fritos. We're talking like 7 A.M. here. He would make fun of me for my bag of almonds and I'd make fun of him for his cholesterol. I do feel like this was good training for what I do now. I have heard literally every joke in the world about how dumb, uppity, and snobby vegan food is. I've heard it while riding around in a giant gas-guzzling truck blasting the air conditioner on the freeway going 90 mph; I've heard it on construction sites surrounded by dudes who were even more rough around the edges than Jerry. I've heard it while sanding down a floor wearing industrial-strength kneepads. COME AT ME, YOUTUBE COMMENTS, because I'VE HEARD IT ALREADY.

And you know what? Jerry had a lot of good points. First off, it's hard to eat well when you're in your car or on job sites all day. Sitting down to a full meal is almost impossible, and you're already so tired you don't want to have to put more work and energy into getting food into your body. Second, you want to eat something you actually *like.* You don't want to have a Tupperware full of something that you're dreading eating, because then you'll just eat half of it and either end up at a drive-through or running down the candy aisle, guns blazing.

One of the best things we can do for our bodies and minds is to focus on nourishing them. I don't mean that in an abstract way, either. Let's be honest, a lot of us have a lot of fear, anxiety, and guilt about food. With all these tricky emotions involved, it's easy to become obsessive about food, bargaining with oneself about what to eat or admonishing oneself for eating the wrong things. First of all, THAT IS EXHAUSTING, and second of all, you deserve better.

When you start thinking about what foods you want to eat in order to best support your body and mind (you're on the same team, remember?), you start to feel more taken care of, less panicked, and more nourished.

PLZ FOR THE LOVE OF GOD BODY GET BETTER SOUP
AKA INSTANT NOODLES (JUST ADD HOT WATER!)

raw • 1 serving

YOU KNOW THAT "UH-OH, I haven't been sleeping or drinking any water or eating any vegetables and now my throat feels sore—OH GOD I CAN'T GET SICK I DON'T HAVE TIME TO BE SICK" feeling? Yeah. Reach for this.

It's super simple. Just throw the ingredients in the jar before you run out the door, then add hot water when you get to school or work. It's also packed with vitamins and minerals that your body needs to stay healthy and productive.

You don't need to use everything in this recipe—just put in what you have on hand. Kelp noodles are admittedly a little weird at first—they don't have a lot of flavor, but they have a nice little crunch and are a rich source of all those minerals your body is craving.

Active time: 5 minutes
Inactive time: 20 minutes

3 or 4 dried mushrooms

1 cup kelp noodles

2 tablespoons kimchi or sauerkraut

½ teaspoon miso paste (or vegetarian bouillon paste)

¼ cup arame or hijiki seaweed

2 tablespoons chopped scallion

1 teaspoon grated fresh ginger

1 teaspoon chopped garlic

Juice of 1 lemon

Hot water

1. Soak the mushrooms in room-temperature water for at least 20 minutes, then give them a quick rinse to remove any residual grit; drain well.

2. Put the mushrooms and all the remaining ingredients except the water in a pint-sized glass jar.

3. Add enough hot water to fill the jar and let sit for 1 to 2 minutes, stirring occasionally.

4. Drink straight from the jar or eat with a spoon.

RAW. VEGAN. NOT GROSS.

KALE CHIPS

mostly raw • 4 servings, or enough for
1 hungry person (aka me)

THIS WAS THE FIRST RECIPE VIDEO I ever did for Tastemade. I was terrified. If you watch the video, you'll see me looking like a sweaty frizzy-haired deer in the headlights. That's because I had done my own hair and makeup (not my strong suit) and also didn't have anyone helping me in the kitchen, so I was running to the prep kitchen to wash dishes in between takes. And there were a lot of takes, because I messed up a lot. I had no idea what I was doing. I went home that night and cried. Then I went back the next day to do it all over again.

The video certainly wasn't my best work, but I still stand by the recipe! These kale chips are a seriously addictive snack and are a great way to eat your leafy greens on the go.

Active time: 15 minutes
Inactive time: 20 minutes or 12 hours

1 cup walnuts, soaked in water overnight

1 bell pepper

½ cup nutritional yeast

¼ cup maple syrup

2 tablespoons fresh lemon juice

½ teaspoon salt

½ teaspoon ground cayenne

1 bunch kale, stems removed

1. Drain the soaked walnuts.

2. Place the walnuts in a food processor, add all the remaining ingredients except the kale, and pulse until the mixture is fully incorporated.

3. Place the kale leaves in a bowl, add the walnut mixture, then massage the mixture into the leaves for a few minutes until the leaves are well coated.

4. Spread the coated leaves on a dehydrator sheet or on a baking sheet lined with parchment paper. Dehydrate overnight or bake in the oven at 200°F until crispy, about 20 minutes.

COLLARD GREEN WRAPS WITH
SPICY DIPPING SAUCE

raw • 4 servings

THIS IS YOUR NEW GO-TO LUNCH. It's packed with colorful, nutrient-dense vegetables and is basically a salad you can eat with your hands. I like to make a big batch of the dipping sauce to keep in my fridge so that if I get home and I'm starving, I can just dip whatever veggies I have on hand to tide me over while I'm making dinner.

Active time: 45 minutes

For the wraps:

4 collard leaves, raw or blanched

For the filling:

1 carrot, peeled and julienned

1 bell pepper, julienned

1 jicama, peeled and julienned

½ cucumber, julienned

½ cup shredded cabbage

½ avocado, sliced

For the dipping sauce:

1 (2-inch) piece fresh ginger, peeled

1 large tomato

¼ cup fresh lemon juice

¼ cup almond butter

3 cloves garlic

1 teaspoon ground cayenne

3 scallions, including white and about 3 inches of green

2 tablespoons maple syrup, agave, or raw honey

1 tablespoon sesame oil

1. Place the collard leaves on your cutting board.

2. Place a few of each julienned vegetable and a small bunch of cabbage on the center of each leaf and top with a slice of avocado.

3. Fold the bottom of the collard green over the vegetables, then fold in the sides and keep rolling it up like a burrito until it's closed. Set aside.

4. Make the dipping sauce: Blend all the ingredients in a blender or food processor. Serve on the side.

TO GO

IMMUNITY BOWL

cooked • 2 servings

I LOVE MAKING THESE BECAUSE it feels like a game to me: How many nutritious things can I get in one bowl? I recommend taking a couple of hours on a Sunday to make a big batch of quinoa, roast some beets or sweet potatoes, or grill some asparagus or whatever else you have left over in your fridge. If you have all of these components on hand, you can pull together a satisfying and savory meal in less than five minutes whenever you need some nourishment.

Active time: 10 minutes
Inactive time: 20 minutes

½ cup quinoa (preferably soaked in water overnight)

½ teaspoon salt

¼ cup wakame or arame seaweed

3 to 4 cups spinach leaves

1 cup julienned carrot

¼ cup fresh cilantro leaves

1 avocado, sliced

Quick Pickled Veggies (recipe follows)

For the dressing:

¼ cup tahini

2 tablespoons apple cider vinegar

1 tablespoon tamari

1 clove garlic, minced

Pinch of salt

1. Rinse and drain the quinoa. Put it in a pot with the salt and 1 cup water (1¼ cups if the quinoa was not soaked). Bring to a boil, cover, and reduce to a simmer; cook until the water has been absorbed, 15 to 20 minutes.

2. While the quinoa is cooking, soak the seaweed for about 10 minutes and then drain.

3. Whisk the dressing ingredients together in a small bowl.

4. Place the quinoa, spinach, and seaweed in serving bowls. Add the carrot, cilantro, and avocado. Add quick pickled veggies, drizzle with dressing, and serve.

QUICK PICKLED VEGGIES

raw • 2 or 3 pint-size jars

Active time: 15 minutes
Inactive time: 24 hours to 3 days

¾ cup fresh citrus juice
(equal parts lemon,
orange, and grapefruit)

¼ cup white wine
vinegar

1 teaspoon kosher salt

1 teaspoon black
peppercorns

1 teaspoon coriander
seeds

1 teaspoon red pepper
flakes

Carrots, cucumbers,
mushrooms, and/or
cabbage, peeled, if
needed, and sliced or
chopped

1. Combine the citrus juice, vinegar, salt, peppercorns, coriander, and red pepper flakes in a bowl and stir.

2. Pour the liquid over the vegetables in a bowl and let stand for 10 to 15 minutes.

3. Serve immediately, or transfer to a glass jar and put the lid on. They will be even better in 3 days and will last in the fridge for up to 1 month.

NORI HANDROLLS

raw • 2 handrolls

I LIKE THESE BECAUSE they have their own little containers, so they don't get all over your hands while you are running out the door with them. Feel free to add anything you like—I love adding hummus or guacamole to make them more substantial.

Active time: 30 minutes

For the sauce:

¼ cup tahini

2 tablespoons fresh lemon juice

1 tablespoon tamari

1 teaspoon miso

For the handrolls:

2 sheets nori

½ cup shaved red cabbage

½ cup julienned peeled cucumber

½ cup julienned carrot

½ cup julienned jicama

½ avocado, sliced

1. Make the sauce: Whisk or blend all the ingredients with 2 to 3 tablespoons water in a food processor until smooth (you may need to add additional water—the sauce should be smooth and creamy).

2. Make the handrolls: Place a nori sheet flat on a cutting board, fill one corner with half of the veggies, drizzle with sauce, then roll into a little cone. Repeat with the second nori sheet.

3. Eat as is, and use extra sauce for dipping.

CREAMY JICAMA SALAD

raw • 2 servings

I'M JUST NOT A POTATO SALAD PERSON.
I think it's partly because I always remember some kid getting food poisoning from it after going to a school picnic where it got left out in the sun too long.

This is a lot different from your standard potato salad, starting with the fact that it doesn't actually have any potatoes in it. The jicama replaces the texture and sweetness of the potatoes. I love adding a bunch of tarragon and dill in there, but feel free to add some basil, parsley, or even rosemary—all would be delicious.

Active time: 30 minutes

3 cups diced jicama

½ cup diced celery

½ cup diced red onion

Pinch of sea salt

For the dressing:
2 tablespoons tahini

½ avocado, peeled

1 tablespoon Dijon mustard

1 tablespoon fresh lemon juice

½ teaspoon tamari

½ teaspoon ground cumin

1 clove garlic, minced

1 tablespoon chopped fresh dill, plus more for garnish

1 tablespoon chopped fresh tarragon, plus more for garnish

1. Mix the jicama, celery, and onion in a large bowl, sprinkle with the salt, and set aside while you make the dressing.

2. Make the dressing: Blend all the ingredients in a blender, adding up to ¼ cup water as needed to get a smooth consistency.

3. Pour the dressing over the salad mixture and toss. Garnish with extra dill and tarragon.

WATER HACKS

raw

I am pretty much constantly dehydrated, so I have to find ways of tricking myself into drinking more water. Obviously it's important to keep my water bottle with me, but I've found that if I know I'm giving my body an extra boost of nutrition and keep the flavors interesting, I'm more likely to drink water. Here are a few things that I keep in my bag at all times, so that when I get to wherever I'm going, I'm more apt to refill my water bottle and pop one of these feel-good boosters in!

FEELING BLOATED?

½ lemon

Lemon is alkalinizing to the body (you want that!), boosts immunity, aids digestion, and keeps skin clear and glowing. It is also high in pectin fiber, which helps fight hunger cravings and can aid in weight loss. I either bring a whole lemon with me and cut it up with my pocket knife, or I drop a slice of it in my water bottle before I run out the door.

DIGESTION OUTTA WHACK?

1 tablespoon chia seeds

Chia seeds are a great source of fiber, calcium, iron, and omega-3 fatty acids. They also slow the digestion of carbohydrates, which helps give the body long-lasting energy. I keep a little zip-top bag of them in my purse, and they have saved me many times when I've found myself stranded and starving—they are surprisingly filling!

ACHY JOINTS?

pinch of turmeric

Turmeric has powerful anti-inflammatory and antioxidant properties, and is proven to help brain function. If I have hot water, I'll make a tea with the root, but otherwise I just sprinkle a little bit of ground turmeric in my water for a yellow tint that makes people wonder what the heck I'm drinking.

FIGHTING OFF A BUG?

7 drops oregano oil

Not gonna lie: It's not my favorite tasting supplement, but oregano oil is some powerful stuff! Just a few drops in your water gives you one of the best lines of defense against all forms of infection. Studies have revealed its ability to fight food-borne illnesses, upper respiratory and urinary tract infections, and both yeast and parasitic infections. I keep a small bottle in my purse and put a few drops in my water when I remember.

PROTEIN-PACKED GRANOLA BARS

mostly raw • 10 bars

THESE LITTLE DUDES are naturally salty-sweet, super moist, and amazing for snacking on the fly. They also require zero baking—just ten minutes of assembly and then some time in the fridge to set up. They're packed with protein, essential fatty acids, fiber, vitamins, and minerals that will tide you over until you can get to your next meal.

Active time: 10 minutes
Inactive time: 15 to 20 minutes

1 cup pitted dates

½ cup almond butter

¼ cup maple syrup

2 cups gluten-free oats

¼ cup hemp seeds

¼ cup cacao nibs

2 tablespoons chia seeds

1. Blend the dates, almond butter, and maple syrup in a food processor for about 30 seconds, until the big chunks are gone.

2. In a large bowl, combine the oats, hemp seeds, cacao nibs, and chia seeds and mix. Add the date mixture and stir to coat.

3. Line an 8-inch square baking dish or other small pan with parchment paper so the bars lift out easily.

4. Spread the oat mixture in the prepared dish and press down until uniformly flattened. Cover with parchment paper and set in the refrigerator or freezer for 15 to 20 minutes to harden.

5. Remove from the pan and cut into 10 bars. Store in an airtight container in the fridge or freezer for up to a few days.

APPLE RINGS

raw • 24 rings

IT'S ALWAYS GOOD TO HAVE a quick little sweet treat on hand. Feel free to thread these into a necklace to sneak some snacks into the movie theater.

Active time: 10 minutes
Inactive time: 45 minutes or 3 hours

4 to 5 apples

1 teaspoon cinnamon

½ teaspoon ground ginger

½ teaspoon freshly grated nutmeg

1. Core the apples, then slice them into rings on a mandoline (or slice them thinly with a knife).

2. Toss with the spices.

3. Spread the apples out on a dehydrator sheet and dehydrate for 3 to 4 hours, or bake on a parchment-lined baking sheet at 200°F for 45 minutes to 1 hour. Store in an airtight container for up to a week.

SALADS

I got my first job as soon as I turned sixteen. A restaurant had just opened about a mile from my house (which was a miracle in and of itself, because there wasn't even a corner store within about five miles). Our neighbor, Ron Nicoli, was a renaissance man. He raised cattle. (He named one after me! Laura the cow! Then he ate her.) My dad used to bring home trailers full of Ron's "black gold"—a soil he'd created out of garden compost and horse manure. The stuff could grow anything. Ron was also an amazing Italian cook and a contractor, and he just so happened to open a restaurant right as I was turning sixteen and could legally work.

On my very first day, I spilled an entire tray of drinks on a seventy-year-old woman, and . . . wait for it . . . it was her birthday party! She was very gracious about it, thank God, and I recovered from the trauma and went on to become a pretty badass little server. I loved the job because it forced my introverted angsty teenage self to be extroverted and borderline hammy.

It was a very small restaurant, and I wore a lot of hats. For some reason the servers were responsible for making the salads for our tables (which I later learned was definitely not up to health code standards!), but I liked working with food, so I didn't mind. The chef had come up with all kinds of combinations that I had never thought of. He added fruit and cooked squash and seeds, and made all his own dressings. (At that point I had only really had bottled Hidden Valley Ranch, so that alone opened my eyes.) I learned that it takes only a few fresh ingredients to make a salad work.

TOMATO POMEGRANATE SALAD

raw • 4 or 5 servings

THE ONE THING YOU MUST know is that you need fresh, ripe tomatoes for this recipe. Sad, mealy, out-of-season tomatoes just won't work. And don't worry about them turning into a big sloppy mess; we're going to slice and then salt them, and then let them drain for about 30 minutes. The salt will pull the moisture out and intensify the flavor.

I love pomegranate seeds on top because they add a bit of extra crunch and sweetness. There are a lot of YouTube videos out there with hacks for how to get pomegranate seeds out the fastest, but my go-to is to seed them with the fruit submerged in a big bowl of water. This helps me to not stain everything I own, and also makes it easy to collect the seeds, as they just sink to the bottom of the bowl.

Active time: 10 minutes
Inactive time: 30 minutes

8 to 10 medium tomatoes

Salt

¼ cup olive oil

1 tablespoon white wine vinegar

2 cloves garlic, grated

1 pomegranate

Freshly ground black pepper

1. Cut the tomatoes into ½-inch slices, place in a colander, sprinkle with a few healthy pinches of salt, and let sit and drain for about 30 minutes.

2. While the tomatoes are doing their thing, combine the oil, vinegar, and garlic in a small bowl. Set aside, and now get to work at seeding that pomegranate.

3. Transfer the tomatoes to a large bowl (no need to rinse; a lot of the salt has dripped off with the moisture by now). Pour the dressing over the tomatoes and gently mix. Add the pomegranate seeds and a little pepper and serve.

CARROT SALAD WITH LEMON-POPPY SEED DRESSING

mostly raw • 4 servings

I LOVE USING DIFFERENT COLORED heirloom carrots, but any fresh carrots you can find will do just fine. You can use a mandoline or just a plain old vegetable peeler to get thin crisp strips. The dressing is sweet and tangy with a citrusy punch. It's so good that I usually make a big batch and just keep it in a glass jar in the fridge for a few days to use on salads and to dip veggies.

Active time: 10 minutes

5 carrots, washed and shaved into thin strips

Handful of fresh cilantro leaves

¼ cup pistachios, coarsely chopped

For the dressing:

¼ cup olive oil

1 tablespoon maple syrup

2 tablespoons poppy seeds

1 teaspoon grated fresh ginger

Grated zest of 1 lemon

Juice of 2 lemons

Pinch of salt

1. Put the carrots, cilantro, and pistachios in a large salad bowl.

2. Make the dressing: Put the oil, maple syrup, poppy seeds, ginger, lemon zest, and lemon juice in a blender and pulse until well combined.

3. Pour the dressing over the salad and toss, finishing with a pinch of salt.

SHAVED ASPARAGUS SALAD WITH LEMON TARRAGON DRESSING

raw • 4 servings

I HAD NO IDEA THAT you could eat asparagus raw, so the first time I saw a ribboned asparagus salad (at a traditional restaurant, no less), I was pumped. I knew I needed to go home to try my own version. I find that it's even better the day after I've made it, as the flavors have had more time to develop.

Active time: 20 minutes

1 pound asparagus
(10 to 12 stalks)

2 cups arugula or
mustard greens

2 cups snow peas,
trimmed

1 beet, shaved on a
mandoline or cut
into thin matchsticks

For the dressing:

2 tablespoons fresh
lemon juice

¼ cup olive oil

2 shallots, thinly sliced

2 tablespoons tarragon,
chopped

1 clove garlic, crushed

1. Lay an asparagus stalk on its side on a cutting board. Starting at the tough end, use a vegetable peeler to shave off thin asparagus ribbons from stalk to tip, peeling away from the tough end in your hand. Continue with the rest of the asparagus. You'll have leftover stalk nubs; just get rid of those.

2. Put the asparagus, arugula, snow peas, and beet in a large salad bowl.

3. Make the dressing: In a small bowl, combine all the ingredients.

4. Pour the dressing over the salad and toss.

SEA VEGGIE SALAD

mostly raw • 4 servings

I HAVE TO ADMIT THAT it took me a while to get into seaweed. I hadn't tried it growing up, and the umami flavors were new to me. Once I got used to them, though, I was hooked. It felt like my body had been craving them. Sea veggies are some of the most nutritious foods you can eat, packed with calcium, minerals, iron, protein, vitamin B12, and fiber, all while still being low in calories. These days you can find them in most health food stores, but you'll find the best selection and prices at your local Asian market.

If you're just getting used to eating seaweed, the dressing can really make or break it for you. This creamy dressing is perfect because it balances out that *Little Mermaid* "Under the Sea" vibe.

Active time: 15 minutes
Inactive time: 10 minutes

½ cup arame seaweed

½ cup wakame seaweed

2 cups arugula

½ cup thinly sliced cucumber

¼ cup cilantro, finely chopped

2 tablespoons minced scallion

For the dressing:

½ cup tahini

½ cup tamari

¼ cup sesame oil

¼ cup maple syrup

1 teaspoon sea salt

1. Soak the arame and wakame in fresh cool water. When they have expanded and softened, after 5 to 10 minutes, drain thoroughly. Gently squeeze to remove excess water. Slice into $1/3$-inch strips.

2. Combine the seaweeds, arugula, cucumber, cilantro, and scallion in a large bowl.

3. Make the dressing: Blend all the ingredients either by hand in a small bowl or in a blender.

4. Drizzle the dressing on top of the salad and toss.

ORANGE-WATERCRESS SALAD

raw • 4 servings

I WAS IN LINE AT a grocery store once, holding an obscene amount of basil, and the very nice lady behind me commented on how beautiful and fresh it looked. She asked me what I was using it for. "Just a pesto," I shrugged. "Oh, you should try it in salad. I put fresh herbs in all my salads—it tricks people into thinking I'm a good cook!"

These days, I rarely make a salad without throwing a few herbs in. I recommend keeping a few little plants in your kitchen so you can just tear off a few leaves anytime you want them. Freshly picked herbs add fresh flavors and aromas that make people think you've just picked all your ingredients from your very own sustainably harvested garden.

Active time: 15 minutes

2 bunches watercress, cut into 1-inch pieces

2 oranges, peeled and suprêmed

1 avocado, diced

1 bunch fresh mint, finely chopped

1 bunch fresh basil, finely chopped

For the dressing:

¼ cup olive oil

2 tablespoons fresh orange juice

1 tablespoon fresh lemon juice

1 to 2 small shallots, minced

Salt and freshly ground black pepper

1. Put the watercress, oranges, avocado, and herbs in a large salad bowl.

2. Make the dressing: Combine all the ingredients in a glass jar and shake well.

3. Pour the dressing over the salad and toss.

BASIC MASSAGED KALE SALAD

raw • 2 or 3 servings

STILL THINK YOU DON'T like kale? Or maybe you're one of those people who is just pretending to like it to keep up with the cool kids? If either of these applies to you, you need to try massaging your kale. Massaged kale is like kale's cooler older brother—much less bitter (almost sweet!), more tender, and much more in touch with his emotions. A real dreamboat, if you ask me.

Active time: 15 minutes

1 bunch kale

¼ cup fresh lemon juice

¼ cup cold-pressed extra-virgin olive oil

Pinch of sea salt

Small handful of hulled sunflower seeds

1 small pear, shaved into ribbons (optional)

1. Wash, dry, and stem the kale.

2. In a large bowl, dress the kale with the lemon juice and oil and add the salt.

3. With clean hands, grab handfuls of the kale and vigorously rub them together for a few minutes. The leaves will become tender and decrease in volume significantly.

4. Top with the sunflower seeds and pear, if desired, and serve.

HOT PINK KRAUT

raw • about 15 cups

THIS IS BASICALLY A FERMENTED SALAD, but it's also great as a side or condiment on a lot of savory dishes. I can't stress enough how important it is to eat fermented vegetables. They are packed with probiotics that support your immune system, improve digestion, and help your body absorb nutrients from other foods you eat. And if that's not enough, they are also said to lessen seasonal allergies and help clear acne.

Sauerkraut is incredibly easy (and inexpensive) to make. Once you've done this recipe once, you could basically sleepwalk through it. It's that easy.

P.S. If you see mold beginning to form, throw out the batch and start again. Don't stress; it probably just means that some of your equipment was not clean enough.

Active time: 15 minutes
Inactive time: 3 to 10 days

1 large head purple cabbage

2 tablespoons sea salt

About 1 cup grated beet

1 tablespoon juniper berries or caraway seeds (optional)

1. Chop or shred the cabbage and place in a nonreactive bowl.

2. Sprinkle the cabbage with the salt and massage with clean hands until there is plenty of liquid and the cabbage softens (about 10 minutes).

3. Mix in 1 cup beets for every 5 cups cabbage, add the juniper berries, if desired, and mix thoroughly.

4. Stuff the cabbage into a sanitized glass jar, pressing the cabbage so it's submerged in the liquid. If necessary, add a bit of water to ensure all the cabbage is covered. This limits the exposure to air and keeps the sauerkraut from growing mold.

5. Use a smaller sanitized jar filled with beans (or anything else heavy enough!) to help keep the cabbage pressed underneath the liquid. Cover the jars with cheesecloth and secure with a rubber band or twine. Allow the sauerkraut to culture for 3 to 10 days at room temperature (making sure that the kraut doesn't rise above the water level), until it's bubbling and tangy to your liking.

6. Transfer to the refrigerator and have some every day to keep your gut happy!

WATERMELON AVOCADO SALAD

mostly raw • 8 servings

WHEN IT COMES TO FEASTING on watermelon, I can eat anyone under the table. One summer, I was bringing a giant Tupperware of cut watermelon to my office job every day to eat at my desk. I got made fun of a lot for that one—"Watch out, here comes the crazy watermelon lady!" But I didn't care. It's light, hydrating, and it makes me feel like I'm about to jump into a cold mountain lake, even if I'm sitting in an office in the middle of San Francisco.

Active time: 20 minutes

6 cups diced watermelon (about 1 large melon)

2 cucumbers, diced

3 avocados, diced

¼ cup coarsely chopped fresh basil

¼ cup fresh mint leaves

1 tablespoon red pepper flakes

1 teaspoon grated fresh ginger

1 tablespoon maple syrup

1 tablespoon sesame seeds

For the dressing:

¼ cup fresh lime juice

2 tablespoon sesame oil

2 tablespoon olive oil

1 tablespoon tamari

1. Put the watermelon, cucumbers, avocados, basil, and mint in a large salad bowl

2. Make the dressing: Blend all the ingredients in a blender until smooth.

3. Pour the dressing over the salad, then toss. Serve immediately. Leftovers will keep in the refrigerator for a couple of days.

CRISP GREEN APPLE
AND FENNEL SALAD

mostly raw • 6 servings

IN ONE OF MY PAST LIVES I was a park ranger in Marin County. It was mostly taking care of plants, keeping parks safe and clean, and wearing super-unflattering forest green pants. Part of the job was keeping the brush down in fire-prone areas, so I did my fair share of weed whacking. If you've never done it, it's a tedious job because you have to wear a lot of protective gear that makes you hot and sweaty, and you constantly need to replace the wire at the end because it wears out. Still, it was one of my favorite jobs because there was so much wild fennel growing in the area that when I'd hit a patch of it, I'd get hit with a wave of intense fennel aromatherapy. It was intoxicating in the dorkiest way—I loved it.

Every time I make this salad I reminisce about my sweaty weed-whacking days and my super-unflattering forest green ranger pants.

Active time: 20 minutes

3 green apples, cored and thinly sliced

2 bulbs fennel, trimmed and thinly sliced

3 cups baby arugula

1 cup pomegranate seeds

4 chives, chopped

For the dressing:

½ cup tahini

¼ cup fresh lemon juice

2 tablespoons olive oil

1 (1-inch) piece fresh ginger, grated or minced

2 tablespoons maple syrup

½ teaspoon sea salt

1. In a large salad bowl, toss the apple, fennel, and arugula together.

2. Make the dressing: Mix all the ingredients in a small bowl with a fork or in a blender.

3. Pour the dressing over the salad and toss.

4. Divide into six portions and sprinkle each portion with pomegranate seeds before serving. Garnish with chives.

RAW. VEGAN. NOT GROSS.

GINGER SESAME SALAD

mostly raw • 6 servings

THIS DRESSING FEATURES some of my favorite ingredients with the best health benefits. Apple cider vinegar aids digestion by balancing the acid-alkaline environment of the digestive tract. Nutritional yeast is rich in B-complex vitamins that we need to keep our energy up and our stress levels low. Ginger provides great immunity support. Feel free to double up the recipe so that you have some leftover to use throughout the week!

Active time: 20 minutes

For the dressing:

¼ cup sesame oil

½ cup tahini

¼ cup apple cider vinegar

¼ cup maple syrup

1 tablespoon fresh ginger

¼ cup nutritional yeast

½ teaspoon salt

4 sweet peppers, julienned

1 cup jicama, julienned

1 cup carrot, julienned

1 cup summer cabbage, thinly sliced

Handful of mint, thinly sliced

1 tablespoon sesame seeds

1. In a small bowl, mix dressing ingredients.

2. Add all vegetables into large salad bowl, pour dressing over, and toss.

3. Sprinkle sesame seeds over salad before serving.

WEEKNIGHT
DINNERS

When I was about twenty, I went on a five-week mountaineering course in Patagonia, Chile. I had already done a fair amount of backpacking at that point, but this was really next-level OMG-why-did-I-sign-up-for-this-again stuff. Fifteen of us—mostly Chileans and Americans—traveled over remote mountains and glaciers through the Andes Mountains carrying everything we needed on our backs. We had crampons on our shoes and ice axes in our hands, often on four-man rope teams for safety in case someone were to drop into a crevasse that had been covered in snow. It was scary and cold and really physically challenging, but OMG it was so fun, mostly because of the people. It was a crackerjack team of hysterical weirdos who I would otherwise probably never have met.

We really learned the importance of cooking, not just for sustenance, but also as a morale booster when the crew had just battled through a rough, cold, and discouraging day. Having everyone huddled around our tiny stove on the dirt, cooking and eating together, was one of my favorite parts of the trip. I really feel like this can be translated into everyday life. You could have just lived through the Worst Tuesday of All Time, but if you know you can go home and cook and eat with people you love, it makes it all a little easier to endure. Also, I recommend wine.

STUFFED POBLANO PEPPERS
WITH WALNUT CREMA

cooked • 5 peppers

***CHILES EN NOGADA* WAS** a traditional Mexican dish that I first had at my friend Angelica's house. It's poblano peppers stuffed with shredded meat, covered with a walnut cream sauce, and topped with pomegranate seeds, representing all three colors of the Mexican flag: green, white, and red. This is a vegan interpretation of the dish that still reps all the traditional colors.

Active time: 45 minutes
Inactive time: 2 to 3 hours

5 poblano peppers

2 cups walnuts, soaked in water overnight, then drained

2 cups cremini or button mushrooms

1 small white onion, chopped

2 cloves garlic

2 cups cooked brown rice

½ cup fresh cilantro

¾ cup sliced almonds

Salt and freshly ground black pepper

Olive oil

For the walnut crema:

1½ cups walnuts, soaked in water overnight, then drained

About 1 (13.5 ounce) can coconut milk

Pinch of salt

1 cup pomegranate seeds

1. Preheat the oven to 425°F.

2. On a baking sheet, roast the peppers until the skin is blackened, then place in a bowl, cover with plastic wrap, and let sit for 10 to 15 minutes.

3. Once the peppers have steamed, carefully peel away all the skin, leaving the body intact. Make a slit down the middle of each pepper and discard the core and seeds.

4. In a food processor, combine the walnuts, mushrooms, onion, and garlic and blend until a chunky paste forms.

5. Using a spatula, combine this paste with the rice, mixing until well incorporated. Fold in the cilantro, almonds, and salt and pepper to taste.

6. Stuff each pepper with the filling, then use a toothpick or skewer to hold the slit closed. Return the peppers to the baking sheet.

7. Drizzle the peppers with oil and bake for 10 to 15 minutes, until the peppers are wrinkly and starting to brown along the edges.

8. Make the walnut crema: Put all the ingredients in a food processor and blend until completely smooth. Add more or less coconut milk depending on the desired consistency. Remove the peppers from the oven, drizzle with the walnut crema, and sprinkle with pomegranate seeds.

WALNUTBALLS
IN RED SAUCE

mostly raw • 4 servings

OR AS I LIKE TO CALL IT, Confetti and Beachballs. This is an incredibly satisfying and comforting dinner. The zucchini noodles take on the flavor of the tomato sauce really nicely, and walnutballs, made of nuts, seeds, and vegetables, have a great flavor and texture that you can really sink your teeth into.

Active time: 45 minutes
Inactive time: 1 hour or 12 hours

For the walnutballs:

1 cup walnuts, soaked in water for at least 2 hours and up to overnight

1 cup cauliflower florets

½ cup ground flaxseeds

½ yellow onion, chopped

1 clove garlic, chopped

3 tablespoons olive oil

1 tablespoon apple cider vinegar

¼ cup fresh parsley

2 teaspoons ground cumin

1 tablespoon tamari

½ teaspoon salt

3 cups cremini mushrooms

For the red sauce:

1 cup walnuts, soaked in water overnight

1 cup sun-dried tomatoes, soaked in water for at least 15 minutes and up to 1 hour

1 medium tomato

3 tablespoons fresh lemon juice

3 tablespoons olive oil

1 tablespoon maple syrup

1 teaspoon red pepper flakes

1½ teaspoons salt

1. Make the walnutballs: Drain the walnuts and add all the ingredients except the mushrooms to a food processor; process until finely ground, then add the mushrooms and pulse a few times to combine.

2. Roll the mixture into balls, place on dehydrator sheets, and dehydrate overnight or in the oven on a Silpat sheet or parchment paper for 1 to 2 hours at 200°F.

3. Make the red sauce: Drain the walnuts and sun-dried tomatoes and transfer them with all the remaining ingredients to the food processor. Puree. Serve with walnutballs and spiralized zucchini pasta (recipe follows).

4. Divide the zucchini noodles among 4 serving plates and top each with about ½ cup of the sauce and 2 or 3 walnutballs. Enjoy!

SPIRALIZED ZUCCHINI PASTA

3 to 4 zucchini squash

½ teaspoon salt

Spiralize the zucchini by pushing them through the spiralizer. If you don't have a spiralizer, just use a mandoline or a sharp knife to cut zucchini into very thin strips. Toss with the salt and set aside in a colander to drain.

CAULIFLOWER PIZZA

*raw • 2 servings, or a whole pizza for
1 hungry and/or emotional person*

WHAT'S THAT? You had a rough day and are looking to wind down with some emotional eating? Well, friend, if you've got that I-need-to-eat-an-entire-pizza-tonight fire in your eyes, this is a good way to go.

I should warn you that it's more delicate than regular pizza, so you'll probably end up eating it with a fork, but it's so satisfying and hearty that I don't think you'll mind.

Active time: 20 minutes
Inactive time: 1 hour to 12 hours

For the crust:
2 cups cauliflower florets

¼ teaspoon smoked paprika

2 tablespoons nutritional yeast

1 clove garlic, chopped

2 tablespoons olive oil

1 tablespoon fresh oregano leaves

Pinch of salt

For toppings:
Arugula

Balsamic vinegar

For the tomato sauce:
1 cup sun-dried tomatoes, soaked overnight

1 medium tomato

1 teaspoon red pepper flakes

1 tablespoon fresh lemon juice

3 scallions, thinly sliced

1. Make the crust: Chop the cauliflower into smaller pieces and add them to a food processor, blending until the pieces are small and uniform.

2. Place the cauliflower between two kitchen towels and press down to remove moisture.

3. Return the cauliflower to the food processor and add the remaining ingredients; pulse until well combined.

4. Spread the dough into a large circle on a teflex sheet (making sure not to spread it too thin—about ½-inch is good). Dehydrate overnight, or bake in the oven on a baking sheet lined with parchment paper at 200°F for 1 hour.

5. Prepare the arugula: Drizzle a handful of arugula with vinegar and set aside.

6. Make the tomato sauce: Combine all the ingredients in a blender or food processor and puree until smooth.

7. Remove the crust from the dehydrator or oven, spread the tomato sauce on top, and add the arugula.

PESTO PASTA

raw • 4 servings

I LOVE MAKING PESTO. The second I press the button on the food processor to start blending, the smell of basil takes me straight to food nerd heaven. I realize that cucumbers might seem like a strange choice for the noodles, but just give them a shot. They are actually a great complement to the bright flavor of the pesto!

Active time: 20 minutes

For the noodles:

4 to 5 medium cucumbers

1 tablespoon olive oil

1 tablespoon nutritional yeast

2 teaspoons ground turmeric (for color)

For the pesto:

1½ cups fresh basil leaves

½ cup pistachios

¼ cup olive oil

½ teaspoon salt

1. Spiralize the cucumbers by pushing them through the spiralizer. If you don't have a spiralizer, just use a mandoline or a sharp knife to cut the cucumbers into very thin strips.

2. Place the cucumber in a bowl, then add the oil, nutritional yeast, and turmeric and toss to coat.

3. Make the pesto: Put all the ingredients in a food processor and pulse until combined but still a little chunky.

4. Toss the noodles with the pesto and serve.

COLD AVOCADO-GINGER SOUP

raw • 4 servings

THIS IS THE KIND OF RECIPE that first got me excited about raw food. It just made sense to me that eating foods that were as close to their raw state as possible was the best way to nourish my body and take care of myself. It doesn't hurt that recipes like this are so effortless to make. Creamy, cool, and refreshing—this is the dinner you want to make on a hot August night with a cocktail in one hand.

Active time: 10 minutes

2 avocados, pitted and peeled

2 cucumbers, peeled and coarsely chopped

1 tablespoon minced fresh ginger

Small handful of fresh cilantro leaves

¼ cup fresh lime juice

1 teaspoon salt

1. Puree all the ingredients in a high-speed blender until smooth.

2. Divide among 4 bowls and serve.

WATERMELON-MANGO GAZPACHO

raw • 4 to 6 servings

I LOVE SERVING THIS as a starter when I have a bunch of people over, because I can just pass around jars that my guests can sip while they are still mingling. The sweetness of the mango, spiciness of the ginger, and chunkiness of the watermelon—I could seriously drink this stuff by the gallon.

Active time: 20 minutes

3 cups chopped watermelon, seeded as much as possible, plus 2 cups diced watermelon

1 mango, pitted and peeled

1 cup cucumber, peeled and diced

1 cup diced tomato

1 cup diced red bell pepper

1 jalapeño, seeded and diced

3 scallions, finely chopped

1 tablespoon chopped fresh ginger

Juice of 3 limes

1 teaspoon salt

1. Puree the 3 cups chopped watermelon with the mango in a high-speed blender.

2. Pour the puree into a large serving bowl and add the remaining ingredients.

3. Stir and serve, or refrigerate until ready to serve.

SWEET POTATO ENCHILADAS

cooked • 5 or 6 servings

THIS IS A GOOD ONE for your friends who still can't get down with the vegan thing, thinking it's too wimpy or not filling enough or just plain boring. The tortillas become soft and chewy and soak up all that amazing enchilada sauce in the oven, making a perfectly comforting and hearty dinner for even the most aggressive naysayer. I like to bake the enchiladas on a bed of the extra sweet potato mixture that I sauté in step 2.

Active time: 30 minutes
Inactive time: 30 minutes

For the filling:

1 onion, finely diced

2 cloves garlic, minced

3 to 4 sweet potatoes, cut into small chunks

For the sauce:

2 tablespoons coconut oil

2 cloves garlic, minced

1 small onion, diced

3 to 4 medium tomatoes

3 tablespoons chili powder

1 teaspoon sea salt

1 teaspoon ground cumin

1 tablespoon apple cider vinegar

2 tablespoons gluten-free flour or cornstarch

For assembly and serving:

10 to 12 corn tortillas

Coconut oil cooking spray

¼ cup nutritional yeast

Avocado Crema (recipe page 122)

1. Preheat the oven to 375°F.

2. In a saucepan, sauté the onion, garlic, and sweet potatoes over medium heat until tender, about 8 to 10 minutes.

3. Make the sauce: In a second saucepan, put the coconut oil, garlic, and onion. Stir for a few minutes over medium-high heat, then add the rest of the ingredients and simmer for about 10 minutes. Transfer to a blender and blend until smooth, adding ¾ cup water.

4. Warm the tortillas in a pan over medium heat for a few seconds to make them more pliable, then fill each tortilla with the sweet potato mixture and roll up like a taquito.

5. Place the little taquitos in a baking dish sprayed with coconut oil.

6. Spread the sauce over the filled tortillas.

7. Bake for 15 to 20 minutes, until piping hot, then remove from the oven and sprinkle with nutritional yeast. Serve with Avocado Crema.

continued

AVOCADO CREMA

raw • 5 or 6 servings

You could serve this chunky, as more of a guacamole, or thin it out to make it more of a creamy sauce topping. You could also add diced tomatoes, red onions, or hot peppers once it's been blended.

Active time: 5 minutes

1 large avocado, pitted and peeled	2 tablespoons chopped fresh cilantro
Juice of 1 lime	¼ teaspoon salt, or more to taste

1. Combine all the ingredients and about ¼ cup water in a food processor and process until completely smooth (add more water for a creamier consistency, less for chunkier).

2. Season with additional salt, if needed.

GOLDEN GAZPACHO

raw • 4 or 5 servings

I'LL OFTEN SEE MAGAZINE covers with tempting headlines like "50 Ways to Feel Better NOW" or "How to Get Sexier in Minutes!" and then when I flip to the article, it'll be things like "Wear a bright shade of lipstick" or "Put on a hot pink top!"

As a woman who always has lipstick on my teeth, some of these suggestions don't really work for me, but I do think you can apply—or even improve upon—this principle by using it with food. Like, if you're feeling crappy, why not try to eat the brightest and most colorful meal you can? As long as they aren't Jolly Ranchers, you're probably going to feel better. Like, actually feel better.

Active time: 20 minutes
Inactive time: 2 to 3 hours

4 to 5 yellow heirloom tomatoes

2 cups peeled and coarsely chopped cucumbers

2 yellow bell peppers, chopped

1 onion, coarsely chopped

2 cloves garlic, chopped

¼ cup fresh basil, plus more for garnish

1 teaspoon salt

¼ cup olive oil

2 tablespoons apple cider vinegar

1. Place all the ingredients in a large bowl and toss well, then put in the refrigerator and allow everything to marinate for a few hours.

2. Transfer the mixture to a blender and puree until completely smooth.

3. Divide among 4 or 5 serving bowls, garnish with basil, and serve.

SWEET POTATO CURRY

cooked • 4 servings

ACCORDING TO THE principles of Ayurveda, we need warming spices and foods in the cold winter months in order to balance our immune systems and stay healthy. Curry contains spices like ginger, mustard seeds, cayenne, cinnamon, and nutmeg, which all heat the body. The quality of curry powders can vary greatly, so make sure you get a high-quality blend.

Active time: 1 hour

2 tablespoons coconut oil

3 cloves garlic, minced

3 tablespoons grated fresh ginger

3 tablespoons Madras curry powder

1 large onion, cut into 2-inch chunks

2 large carrots, cut into 2-inch chunks

2 large sweet potatoes, cut into 2-inch chunks

Salt and freshly ground black pepper

1 pound green beans, trimmed and halved

2 (13.5 ounce) cans coconut milk

Cooked brown rice

Chopped fresh cilantro

1. Put the coconut oil in a sauté pan over medium-high heat. Add the garlic, ginger, and curry powder and stir with a wooden spoon, being careful not to let the garlic burn.

2. Add the onion and let it sweat for 10 minutes, or until translucent.

3. Add the carrots and sweet potatoes and season with salt and pepper.

4. Sauté for another 10 minutes, until slightly softened, then stir in the green beans.

5. Add the coconut milk and stir. Bring to a boil, then reduce the heat to maintain a simmer, cover, and cook for 15 minutes.

6. Serve with brown rice, garnished with cilantro.

ASPARAGUS SOUP

cooked • 4 or 5 servings

MOST ASPARAGUS SOUP recipes are doused with cream, which not only makes them less healthy, but also buries the flavor of fresh spring asparagus. This soup is thickened up with the addition of sweet potatoes. It's super creamy and perfect for a brisk spring evening.

Active time: 45 minutes

2 onions, diced

3 tablespoons coconut oil

2 cloves garlic, chopped

4 large sweet potatoes, cut into small chunks

6 cups vegetable stock or water

2 bunches asparagus, tough ends removed, stalks cut into ½-inch pieces

1 teaspoon salt

Cashew Sour Cream (recipe follows)

1. In a large saucepan, sauté the onions in the coconut oil over medium heat until translucent, about 5 minutes.

2. Add the garlic, sweet potatoes, and stock, bring to a boil, then lower the heat and allow to simmer for about 15 minutes.

3. Add the asparagus and continue to simmer until it's completely tender, about 10 minutes.

4. Transfer to a high-speed blender and blend until completely smooth.

5. Pour through a strainer back into the saucepan to make sure you catch any leftover strings from the asparagus. Reheat and ladle into individual serving bowls.

6. Place a dollop of the Cashew Sour Cream atop each bowl of soup and serve.

CASHEW SOUR CREAM

raw • 2 cups

Active time: 5 minutes

½ cup raw cashews, soaked in water for at least 1 hour and up to overnight

1 cup fresh coconut meat

3 tablespoons fresh lemon juice

3 tablespoons apple cider vinegar

1 teaspoon sea salt

Blend all the ingredients with 1 cup water in a high-speed blender, adding more water if needed, until it is completely smooth.

SPAGHETTI SQUASH
MAC AND CHEESE

cooked • 4 servings

NO, THIS DOESN'T TASTE LIKE the heaven that resides inside the blue box. But it also won't make you feel as sluggish, cranky, or hungry 10 minutes after you eat it. It's packed with fiber and some healthy fat to keep your belly happy and full.

Active time: 20 minutes
Inactive time: 1 hour

1 spaghetti squash

drizzle of olive oil

2 tablespoons coconut oil

1 shallot, diced

2 garlic cloves, minced

¼ cup nutritional yeast

1 teaspoon turmeric (for color)

juice of 1 lemon

¼ teaspoon ground nutmeg

1 cup cashews, soaked at least 1 hour and up to overnight

1. Halve the spaghetti squash, scoop out the seeds, place faceup on a cookie sheet and drizzle with olive oil. Cook at 400°F for 30 to 45 minutes.

2. Allow to cool, then use a fork to scrape out the spaghetti strands, moving your fork in the same direction as the strands. Set aside while you make your cheese sauce.

3. Heat coconut oil in a nonstick pan over medium heat. Add shallots and simmer until they become translucent, then add garlic and cook for 2 to 3 minutes. Add all remaining ingredients (except cashews) and cook for a few more minutes at low heat.

4. Transfer mixture to your blender, add in drained cashews, then blend for about 1 minute or until it's fully smooth.

5. Put the spaghetti squash and cheese mixture into an oven-safe dish and toss until combined.

6. Place back in the oven for 10 to 15 minutes, until heated completely through. Serve warm.

PARTY FOOD

I love having dinner parties, but I have a bad habit of planning them at the very last minute. It'll be around 2 P.M. on a Saturday, and all of a sudden I'll decide that I need to have people over, like, now. I start texting folks (we're talking ten to twelve people, usually) before I realize that my house is a total disaster and I have zero food to feed them. Luckily, I am a fast cleaner, a whiz in the grocery store, and— most important—I'm inviting my friends. They already know I'm disorganized and insane.

I finally hosted my first official "supper club" last year, which is essentially a pop-up restaurant. It was in my friend James Tucker's letterpress shop in San Francisco's Mission District, surrounded by three-thousand-pound German Heidelberg presses. It was a five-course raw vegan dinner for fifty people. I had helpers that day, but I did all the prep myself—the decorations, the photo booth props (cardboard cutouts shaped like pieces of fruit), and, of course, all the food.

I made a wall installation out of dahlias from my parents' garden, and put more on the tables. I made a rose water face spray that said "spray on your neighbor," which we put on the tables to encourage conversation. (In hindsight, that was super weird, but so fun.) Both of my older sisters, my parents, and my grandma came (my grandma took a photo with her head in the grapes cardboard cutout!).

It was insane, but amazing. And just like my parties, my party food is fun, colorful, and able to roll with the punches. Just ask Grandma!

RAW. VEGAN. NOT GROSS.

SPICY MANGO CHILE WRAPS

mostly raw • 6 to 8 servings

I UNINTENTIONALLY MADE THESE for my now husband on our first date. (Oh: I forgot to tell you. I got married. Cool, huh?) I say unintentionally because I hadn't planned on making anything—we were supposed to go out to dinner. But when he came over I got really awkward and nervous, so in order to keep my hands busy and avoid eye contact, I went into autopilot and started making these in the kitchen while we were talking. He loved the bright and crunchy fresh veggies and the hearty filling, which I was particularly happy about, seeing as he isn't even vegan.

Active time: 30 minutes

For the filling:

1 tablespoon sesame oil

¼ cup maple syrup

½ teaspoon salt

¼ cup almond butter

1 tablespoon nama shoyu

2 tablespoons chopped fresh ginger

¼ cup fresh lemon juice

½ cup walnuts

1 to 2 tablespoons red pepper flakes

1 cup raw cashews

For assembly:

½ head cabbage, leaves separated and left whole

1 carrot, julienned

1 bell pepper, julienned

1 cup julienned jicama

1 mango, peeled and thinly sliced

Handful of bean sprouts

1. Make the filling: In a high-speed blender or food processor, puree all the ingredients except the cashews.

2. Add the cashews and pulse a few times, but keep it chunky.

3. Assemble the wraps: Lay out a cabbage leaf and place a few tablespoons of the filling vertically down the center. Arrange the carrot, bell pepper, jicama, mango, and some sprouts on top, then fold the sides in and serve.

MANGO AND COCONUT JICAMA TACOS

raw • 4 to 6 servings

MY FRIEND SOPHIA IS a painter and also a food stylist for the "Raw. Vegan. Not Gross." show. She grew up spending every summer with her grandparents in Guadalajara, Mexico. After she mentioned having had jicama tacos from a few restaurants there, I immediately forced her to tell me everything about them. This is the raw vegan interpretation of them. I love that the jicama has more of a starring role as the taco shell, not just an afterthought that's tossed into the filling. They are so bright and fresh.

Active time: 20 minutes

1 jicama, peeled, root end cut off

1 fresh coconut

4 ripe mangos, peeled and cut into 1-inch chunks

Juice of 1 lime

¼ cup chopped fresh cilantro

Salt

Pineapple Salsa (page 138)

Chipotle Crema (page 138)

1. Using a mandoline, thinly slice the jicama into rounds. These are the taco "shells."

2. Remove the coconut meat from the coconut and cut it into 1-inch pieces.

3. Combine the mangos, coconut, lime juice, cilantro, and salt to taste and fill the jicama taco shells with the mixture.

4. Serve with Pineapple Salsa and Chipotle Crema.

continued

Mango and Coconut Jicama Tacos, continued

PINEAPPLE SALSA
raw • about 4 cups

Active time: 5 minutes

3 cups finely diced
ripe pineapple

½ red onion,
finely diced

1 serrano pepper,
finely diced

Juice of 1 lime

¼ cup chopped
fresh cilantro

Sea salt

Combine all the ingredients in a bowl and
mix well.

CHIPOTLE CREMA
raw • about 1 cup

Active time: 5 minutes

1 cup raw cashews,
soaked in water
overnight and drained

¼ cup canned chipotle
peppers in adobo

1 tablespoon apple
cider vinegar

Salt

Put all the ingredients in a blender and blend
until completely smooth, adding water as
needed.

FRESH VEGGIE TOSTADOS

raw • 6 to 8 servings

THE CRISPY CORN TORTILLAS can either be served whole like a tostada, or broken up and used as chips to scoop the toppings, so don't stress if they break apart while they're dehydrating. They are really delicious either way.

Active time: 30 minutes
Inactive time: 1 hour or 12 hours

For the tortillas:

3 cups fresh corn kernels

1 tablespoon fresh lime juice

1 red bell pepper, chopped

½ onion, chopped

1 tablespoon chili powder

1½ teaspoons salt

1 teaspoon ground cumin

½ teaspoon ground cayenne

2 tablespoons nutritional yeast

¾ cup finely ground flaxseeds

For the topping:

3 Roma (plum) tomatoes, cut into 1-inch chunks

2 ripe avocados, peeled and cut into 1-inch chunks

1 cucumber, seeded and cut into 1-inch chunks

1 jalapeño, minced

Juice of 2 limes

2 to 3 tablespoons chopped fresh cilantro

Salt

1. Make the tortillas: Blend all the tortilla ingredients except the flaxseed in a high-speed blender or food processor. Transfer the mixture to a large bowl and stir in the flaxseeds by hand.

2. Spread this mixture in thin 6-inch circles on a teflex sheet or a baking sheet lined with parchment paper. Dehydrate for 4 to 6 hours, or bake in the oven at 200°F for 30 to 40 minutes, until the tortillas are solid enough to flip.

3. Flip your tortillas, then dehydrate for another 4 to 6 hours, or bake for another 30 to 40 minutes.

4. Make the topping: Mix all the ingredients in a bowl and toss well.

5. Serve the tortillas whole as tostadas topped with veggies, or break up for chips to dip into the topping mixture.

ENDIVE SPEARS

mostly raw • 20 to 30 spears

THE CRISP ENDIVE LEAVES pair beautifully with the crunch of the carrots and celery and the creamy sesame miso dressing. These are great finger food at a party because people can eat them with one hand while holding a cocktail in the other.

Active time: 30 minutes

6 endives

2 large carrots, finely diced

5 celery stalks, finely diced, plus celery leaves for garnish

1 large or 2 small shallots, finely diced

¼ cup chopped fresh mint

½ cup pine nuts

⅓ cup Sesame Miso Dressing (recipe follows), plus more for serving

Salt and freshly ground black pepper

1. Cut the stem end off each endive. The leaves will easily loosen and separate into spears.

2. Combine the carrots, celery, shallots, mint, and pine nuts in a bowl and toss lightly with the Sesame Miso Dressing. Add salt and pepper to taste.

3. Spoon the filling into the endive spears.

4. Finish with additional dressing, if desired, and garnish with celery leaves.

SESAME MISO DRESSING

raw • ½ cup

¼ cup miso paste

1 tablespoon sesame oil

1 tablespoon apple cider vinegar

1 teaspoon maple syrup

1 teaspoon tamari

Whisk all ingredients together, adding 1 to 2 tablespoons of water as needed to get a pourable consistency. Lasts up to a week in the fridge.

GINGER-GRAPEFRUIT GRANITA

raw • 6 servings

GRANITA IS THE ADULT VERSION of a snow cone, except better because the flavored syrup doesn't all sink to the bottom. People go crazy for this at parties.

I am obsessed with the grapefruit ginger combination—it's so light and refreshing that I could eat a whole bucket of it. I like to just blend everything up and throw it right in the freezer, but if you want a smoother texture, you can run it through a sieve first to make it smoother.

Active time: 5 minutes
Inactive time: 12 hours

3 cups fresh grapefruit juice

¾ cup agave nectar

2 tablespoons grated fresh ginger

Grated zest of 1 lime

1. Put all the ingredients in a blender and blend until smooth, then pour into a shallow glass dish, cover with plastic wrap, and freeze overnight.

2. Using a fork, scrape the mixture until flakes form. Return to the freezer until ready to serve.

JALAPEÑO-PINEAPPLE GRANITA

raw • 6 servings

LOOK, I'M NOT TELLING YOU that you should add tequila to this, but I'm definitely not telling you that you shouldn't (blend it in with the other ingredients—it'll freeze just fine).

Active time: 5 minutes
Inactive time: 12 hours

2 cups pineapple chunks

Grated zest of 1 lime

¼ cup fresh lime juice

½ jalapeño, seeded

Pinch of salt

1. Put all the ingredients in a blender and blend until smooth, then pour into a shallow dish, cover with plastic wrap, and freeze overnight.

2. Using a fork, scrape the mixture until flakes form. Return to the freezer until ready to serve.

SPRING ROLLS

cooked • 8 servings

ONCE, I HAD BEEN TRYING to prep these spring rolls, but I just straight up ran out of time and realized I wouldn't be able to roll them all. I marched all the ingredients out on cutting boards and laid them down on the dining table and informed my friends that they were responsible for making their own. At first I was embarrassed by my failure to get food on the table, but then I realized that everyone actually loved being able to build their own, because they could customize them and make them exactly how they liked them, and it was a great conversation starter for the folks who didn't know each other that well yet. From now on, I'm only doing BYOSR (build your own spring roll).

There's really no limit to what else you can put in here. I love adding mango and cilantro. Make them your own!

Active time: 30 minutes

8 rice paper spring roll wrappers

1 cup thinly sliced carrots

1 cup thinly sliced cucumber

½ cup thinly sliced yellow bell pepper

1 large bunch fresh basil

1 small bunch fresh mint

For the dipping sauce:

½ cup tamari

2 tablespoons apple cider vinegar

2 tablespoons raw honey or maple syrup

1 tablespoon sesame oil

1 teaspoon minced fresh ginger

1 clove garlic, minced

1 teaspoon red pepper flakes

1. Fill a shallow dish with room-temperature water (just make sure it's a little wider than your rice paper wrappers).

2. Place one wrapper in the water for about 1 minute, until it becomes soft and pliable.

3. Transfer the wrapper to a cutting board and place a small handful of the vegetables and herbs in the center.

4. Fold the top half of the wrapper over the fillings, then fold in both sides, and last, fold the bottom up to seal. Repeat for each spring roll.

5. Make the dipping sauce: Put all the ingredients in a blender and blend until smooth. Transfer to a small bowl and serve alongside the spring rolls.

PAGE 170

DIE ALONE

've had a lot of weird jobs. I've been a park ranger, gas station attendant, furniture refurbisher, line cook, server, and spent the worst day of my life selling phone services door to door. The best job I've ever had, though, was working for a small letterpress company in San Francisco. It was a close-knit team of about ten hilarious, creative, warm, fun, and loving people whom I still consider some of my best friends. After working from home for so long, going to an office every day felt like summer camp. For some reason one April, everything started going wrong for all of us. Christina got hit by a car while she was walking (don't worry, she was fine); Stewey, Lia, and I all broke up with our boyfriends; Lyndsey got kicked out of her house; and then the kicker: We all found out we were losing our jobs because the company was relocating.

Everyone was a bit of a mess emotionally with all the upheaval. The good news is, emotional upheaval is scientifically proven to make hilarious people even funnier. We started doing this thing where anytime someone said something depressing, he or she would follow it up with ". . . whatever, I'm just gonna die alone anyway." Never underestimate the healing power of humor and commiseration.

While I am by no means trying to promote unhealthy coping mechanisms, I will say that sometimes when you feel stressed or low, you will want to stuff your face with some food to make yourself feel better. So why not do it with food that is actually going to nourish and support you and your body, rather than some junk that is going to make you feel worse?

BERRIES WITH MILK

raw • 2 cups

THIS HAS SERVED AS MY DINNER on many a night when my fridge was empty or I was just too tired to prepare a real meal. I don't say this in a holier-than-thou "I'm SO CRAZY I eat SO healthy I just CAN'T HELP IT TEE-HEE" kind of way, either—it's often followed up with a giant bowl of popcorn and/or gluten-free beers aplenty. But you can make this your default "anytime recipe" simply by making sure you always have frozen berries on hand. I buy about ten packages every couple of weeks, which apparently is just enough to make the checkout lady look over her glasses to ask just what I plan to do with all those berries.

Active time: 5 minutes

2 cups frozen blueberries or raspberries

½ cup almond milk, or more if needed

¼ teaspoon stevia, or 1 tablespoon maple syrup

Put the berries into a bowl. Cover with almond milk and optional sweetener, then eat like a bowl of cereal.

WHEN I DIP YOU DIP
WE DIP RANCH

raw • about 2 cups

MY COLLEGE ROOMMATE introduced me to the holy "pizza and ranch" combination, for which I will be eternally grateful. Creamy plus tangy equals crazy delicious. I would put the combo in the "good drunk food" category, but ranch is also a great solo in the good ol' crudité tray!

Active time: 5 minutes

2 cups raw cashews, soaked in water overnight and drained

½ cup fresh lemon juice

1 clove garlic, chopped

1 tablespoon onion powder

1 teaspoon salt

¼ cup minced fresh chives

2 tablespoons minced fresh dill

Put the cashews and all the remaining ingredients in a blender and blend until smooth, adding water to thin if needed.

KEEP YOUR SWEATPANTS ON
TORTILLA PIZZAS

cooked • 1 serving for 1 person in sweatpants

I CONSIDER THESE SWEATPANTS FOOD. The combination of the light crispy crusts with the tangy tomato sauce and creamy "cheese" sauce is so comforting and satisfying. I like snapping pieces off to munch on while I'm standing in my kitchen in a full sweatsuit.

Active time: 10 minutes
Inactive time: 15 minutes

For the tomato sauce:
1 cup sun-dried tomatoes, soaked in hot water for at least 5 minutes and up to 2 hours

1 medium tomato

1 teaspoon red pepper flakes

1 tablespoon fresh lemon juice

3 scallions, thinly sliced

Pinch of salt

For the tortillas:
2 brown rice tortillas

Olive oil

For the cheesy sauce:
½ cup pine nuts or cashews

½ cup hemp seeds

2 teaspoons nutritional yeast

Juice of 1 lemon

Pinch of salt

Optional toppings:
Fresh basil

Fresh oregano

Chopped or sliced tomato

1. Preheat the oven to 350°F.

2. Make the tomato sauce: Put all the ingredients in a blender or food processor and blend until smooth.

3. Coat both sides of each tortilla with a tiny bit of oil. (One of those refillable oil sprayers works great here.)

4. Place the tortillas on a baking sheet, spread a thin layer of the sauce all over, excluding the outer ¹/₂-inch so that it won't spread over the sides while it cooks.

5. Place in the oven and bake for 10 minutes, or until crispy.

6. Meanwhile, make the cheesy sauce: Put all the ingredients in a cleaned blender or food processor with ¹/₄ cup water and blend until smooth.

7. Remove the tortillas from the oven and top with cheesy sauce, adding basil, oregano, and tomatoes, if desired.

EAT YOUR FEELINGS POPCORN

cooked • all your feelings (about 8 cups popped)

SOMETIMES YOU JUST NEED TO dig into a giant bowl of popcorn. Why not do it with popcorn that's heart healthy and not laced with chemicals and trans-fats and all that junk?

Make sure to get organic popcorn kernels, which are super cheap in the bulk section of grocery stores.

Don't be too bummed if you burn the first batch. Once you get the hang of it, it's the easiest and laziest thing in the world to make.

Active time: 10 minutes

3 tablespoons coconut oil

½ cup popcorn kernels

1. Put the coconut oil in a heavy-bottomed pot over medium-high heat.

2. Add a few of the popcorn kernels.

3. When you see one of the kernels pop, add the rest of the kernels and place the lid on the pot.

4. DON'T WALK AWAY! Every few seconds, shake the pot over the stove to prevent the bottom kernels from burning.

5. Continue until you hear a few seconds between pops, about 2 to 3 minutes.

6. Remove from the heat and keep shaking for a few seconds (so you don't get a pop to the face!), then remove the lid and add toppings.

7. I recommend three topping options:

CHEESY POPCORN

¼ cup melted coconut oil

¼ cup nutritional yeast

Pinch of salt

1. Drizzle coconut oil on your popcorn first, in order to help the other toppings stick to the individual kernels.

2. Finish by sprinkling on the nutritional yeast and salt.

CINNAMON-SUGAR POPCORN

¼ cup melted coconut oil

2 teaspoons cinnamon

¼ cup xylitol, stevia, or coconut sugar

Pinch of salt

1. Drizzle coconut oil on your popcorn first, in order to help the other toppings stick to the individual kernels.

2. Finish by sprinkling with cinnamon, your sweetener of choice, and salt.

CARAMEL CORN DRIZZLE

The secret with this caramel is to keep stirring continuously so that it doesn't have a chance to harden before you get it on the popcorn. Biting into a kernel with a bit of hard caramel topping is salty-sweet heaven.

1 cup coconut sugar

6 cups popped popcorn

Pinch of sea salt

1. Heat the coconut sugar in a saucepan over low heat, stirring continuously until it melts to become caramel.

2. Immediately drizzle the caramel over the popcorn and sprinkle with salt.

I NEED TO MUNCH MINDLESSLY
BRUSSELS SPROUT CHIPS

raw • 3 to 4 cups

YOU'LL LOVE CHOWING DOWN on a big bowl of these light and airy little leaves; they have just a touch of salt and a little bit of a kick. The hardest part of this recipe is actually getting the leaves off the little bulbs. I like to do this with a friend while sipping wine. Then you have something to focus on while you chat, and you get a salty snack to nosh on at the end! Win-win, as far as I can tell.

Active time: 20 minutes
Inactive time: 20 minutes or 3 to 4 hours

1 lb. Brussels sprouts (about 20)

2 to 3 tablespoons olive oil

1 to 2 teaspoons chili powder

1 teaspoon cayenne

Salt and freshly ground black pepper

1. Separate the leaves of the Brussels sprouts. I like to pull off as many as I can, and then if they get stuck, cut the bottom off to release the rest.

2. Toss the leaves in a bowl with the oil to coat.

3. Spread them out on a dehydrator sheet or baking sheet, making sure they are not touching one another.

4. Dehydrate for 3 to 4 hours, or bake in the oven at 250°F for about 20 minutes, until crispy.

5. Add the chili powder, cayenne, and salt and pepper to taste immediately after removing from the dehydrator or oven, and toss. Serve warm.

SWEET AND SOUR LIKE MY HEART
TAMARIND BALLS
raw • about 12 balls

THIS RECIPE IS RIDICULOUSLY quick and easy. In fact, the hardest part of this recipe might be getting your hands on some tamarind. Tamarind is nature's sweet-and-sour candy. You can usually find some at Asian grocery stores, or you can just look online. If you can't find the pods, look for tamarind paste or pulp.

Active time: 20 minutes
Inactive time: 30 minutes

1 cup tamarind paste or pulp (or straight from the pod, seeds removed)

1½ cups coconut sugar, divided

½ cup shredded coconut

1 to 2 teaspoons ground cayenne

1. Work through the tamarind paste, pulp, or pods with your fingers to double check that there aren't any seeds that have snuck through.

2. Put the tamarind paste and 1 cup coconut sugar in a food processor and process, adding 1 to 2 tablespoons water as needed to create a thick dough.

3. Remove and roll into balls, place on a baking sheet lined with waxed paper, and place in the refrigerator to chill.

4. In a high-speed blender (or the cleaned food processor) blend the coconut, ½ cup coconut sugar, and cayenne.

5. Roll the balls through the coconut mixture to coat.

6. Cover and return to the fridge for at least 30 minutes or until ready to serve.

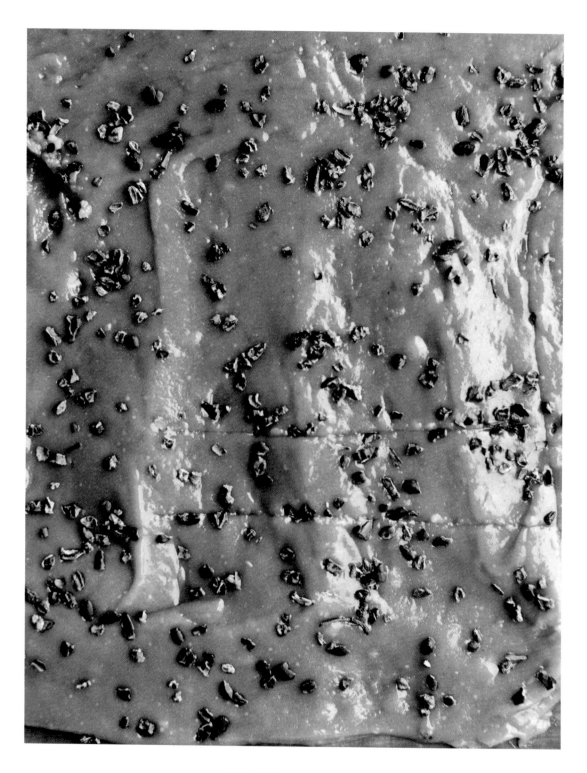

RAW. VEGAN. NOT GROSS.

YES THANKS I'LL HALVAH
THE WHOLE TRAY PLEASE

mostly raw • about 12 slices

HALVAH IS A TAHINI-BASED Middle Eastern confection. It's sold in some bakeries, but most people have only ever seen it wrapped in plastic and sitting on a dusty shelf in a corner store. This version is creamy and fresh, packed with calcium from the sesame seeds and antioxidants from the cacao nibs. If you're feeling really fancy you could even throw in some pistachios or cover it with a chocolate shell (see page 187).

Active time: 10 minutes
Inactive time: 1 hour

2 cups tahini

½ cup maple syrup

¼ cup coconut oil

1 tablespoon vanilla extract

3 tablespoons cacao nibs

1. Combine all the ingredients except the cacao nibs in a food processor, or just mix by hand.

2. Spread the mixture about $^1/_2$-inch thick into a waxed paper–lined 9x12-inch baking pan.

3. Sprinkle the cacao nibs on top.

4. Place in the freezer and allow it to set up for about 1 hour, then cut into 2-inch slices. Keep in the freezer until ready to serve.

SHAKES

mostly raw • 1 shake each

I HAVE SOME VERY SERIOUS nostalgia for those fast-food drive-through milk shakes. I remember always ordering whatever flavor my older sister got because I wanted to be like her, and I remember using my whole body to try to suck the shake up through the straw when it was still too cold and thick. In McD's honor, I've made their three shake flavors. These are every bit as rich and decadent as the originals, but spare you the artificial flavoring, corn syrup, and dairy. I use canned coconut milk because it gives that rich smooth creaminess that I need in a shake.

Active time: 5 minutes

CHOCOLATE SHAKE

1 (13- to 14-ounce) can full-fat coconut milk

¼ cup cocoa powder

¼ cup agave nectar or honey

Pinch of sea salt

1 cup ice

STRAWBERRY SHAKE

1 (13- to 14-ounce) can full-fat coconut milk

½ cup strawberries, fresh or frozen

¼ cup agave nectar or honey

Pinch of sea salt

1 cup ice

VANILLA SHAKE

1 (13- to 14-ounce) can full-fat coconut milk

2 teaspoons vanilla extract

¼ cup agave nectar or honey

Pinch of sea salt

1 cup ice

Blend and serve! Top with coconut whipped cream (page 178) if you're feeling fancy.

DIE ALONE

SWEET POTATO FRIES

cooked • 4 servings

MY SISTER MECHELE IS SOMEONE who doesn't care about sweets, but put a plate of fries on the table and she'll take out your kneecaps to get to them. Personally, I don't trust anyone who says they "don't like sweets," but the good news about sweet potato fries is that they are both salty and sweet, so they make everyone happy!

These fries are also high in fiber, potassium, and iron, all while still having a pretty low glycemic index rating, which means that they'll help prevent those blood sugar spikes that'll lead to sugar cravings later on.

I love adding fresh dill, but these are also delicious with rosemary or oregano.

Active time: 15 minutes
Inactive time: 25 minutes

3 large sweet potatoes

Olive oil

½ cup chopped fresh dill

Sea salt

Beetchup (recipe follows)

1. Preheat the oven to 450°F.

2. Wash and dry the sweet potatoes. Cut each sweet potato in half lengthwise to make it easier to work with. Place the cut side down on the cutting board. Cut lengthwise into quarters. Place the quarters flat-side down and slice to desired thickness.

3. Place in a single layer on a baking sheet and drizzle with oil.

4. Bake for 22 to 25 minutes, flipping them at the halfway point to get even crispiness.

5. Remove from the oven, sprinkle with the dill and sea salt, and serve immediately, with Beetchup.

BEETCHUP

cooked • 3 to 4 cups

You can of course just serve fries with any
old ketchup you have, or you could make
something cool and weird like ketchup made
out of beets. It's got a slightly earthy flavor that
I really like.

Active time: 5 minutes

1 bunch beets, cooked

1 cup apple cider
vinegar

2 tablespoons stone-
ground mustard

⅓ cup maple syrup

¼ teaspoon ground
cumin

1 teaspoon salt

In a food processor, combine all the
ingredients and process until completely
smooth. Store in an airtight container in
the refrigerator for up to 1 week.

SWEETS

In 2011, the private farmers' market where I'd been selling my raw desserts was shut down. I needed to get my business fully legal so that I could sell my food in shops, but that required about ten thousand dollars, which I didn't have. I decided to launch a Kickstarter project to try to crowdsource the money. Keep in mind, I had never done any sort of self-promotion before, so this was incredibly frightening for me. Not only did I have to put myself out there, but I had to ask people for money! I forced myself to say yes to every opportunity to fund-raise, so when a friend of a friend invited me to his "singles dance class" at a Latin dance club in San Francisco, I said yes. The idea was that I would bring samples, explain my Kickstarter, and people would donate. I got there while awkward middle-aged singles were filtering in, and discovered that they didn't have a place for me, so they'd decided that they would put me and my samples on stage under a spotlight. My friend Kendra, seeing how this was all about to play out, leaned in and warned me that this was going to be a "character-building experience." Sweaty folks would come up between dance songs to feast on the chile truffles and lavender macaroons (they loved them!), but people didn't let me get two seconds into my spiel before stuffing a couple of cookies into their mouth and running the other way. At the end of the night, I had given away a ton of desserts, gotten zero donations, and felt like a giant pathetic failure. I cried the whole drive home.

In the end, I did make my Kickstarter goal, but I spent a big chunk of it on sending the rewards out to all my supporters, and by the time I was done I was basically right back where I'd started.

So, look, I'm not a good businesswoman. Definitely don't hire me to help you with your spreadsheets or whatever. But raw desserts? That's my wheelhouse. I can say with confidence that if you make any of the following desserts, you're going to be stoked.

BANANA SOFT SERVE

*raw • 1 to 100 servings, depending
on how many bananas you use*

THIS ONE-INGREDIENT ICE CREAM is another
one of those miracles of the raw food world
that's taken the blogosphere by storm. It's
insanely simple. You're just freezing and then
blending bananas. I have had ex-coworkers,
long-lost family friends, and second cousins
e-mail and text me about this recipe, telling
me that they made it for their roommates/
kids/parents and they couldn't believe it how
easy and delicious it is. It's also great because
as long as you just remember to pick up a few
bananas every time you hit the grocery store,
you'll always have a sweet treat just a few short
steps away. For flavor variations, add in frozen
berries, unsweetened cocoa powder, peanut
butter, or cookie chunks and then blend again.

Active time: 10 minutes
Inactive time: 3 to 4 hours

1-100 Bananas

1. Peel the bananas and cut them into chunks.

2. Place in a glass container or freezer-safe
   bag and freeze until solid.

3. Remove the bananas and blend them in a
   food processor, stopping to smoosh down
   the sides as needed.

BANANA CREAM PIE

mostly raw • 1 pie; 8 to 10 servings

NOT GONNA LIE, banana cream pie was never my first choice at a pie shop. My only reference to the dessert was nerds getting pied in the face in front of their lockers on '90s teen sitcoms. But once I started experimenting with banana cream pie, I realized that it's a dreamy combination of tasty things: a crispy crust, sweet banana filling, dates blended into a perfectly smooth caramel, and creamy coconut whip on top.

Active time: 2 hours
Inactive time: 5 hours or 12 hours

For the crust:

3 cups raw cashews

1 tablespoon coconut oil

3 tablespoons maple syrup

½ teaspoon salt

For the salted caramel:

2 cups pitted Medjool dates, soaked for at least 10 minutes and up to 1 hour

⅓ cup coconut oil

2 tablespoons fresh lemon juice

½ teaspoon salt

1 teaspoon vanilla extract

For the banana filling:

4 frozen bananas

1 tablespoon fresh lemon juice

1 tablespoon coconut oil

Pinch of sea salt

For the coconut whipped cream:

2 (13.5-ounce) cans full-fat coconut milk (no additives or guar gum), chilled in the cans overnight

1. Make the crust: Put the cashews in a food processor and process for about 10 seconds. Add the remaining ingredients and process again, but keep the mixture somewhat chunky.

2. Press the mixture into a 8-inch springform tart pan, making sure to reinforce the sides so they don't break, and dehydrate overnight or bake in the oven at its lowest temperature for 3 to 4 hours or until firm to the touch. (Alternatively, place the crust in the freezer for about 1 hour so that it can firm up—just beware that it'll soften when you bring it back to room temp.)

3. Make the salted caramel: Soak the dates for at least 10 minutes and up to 1 hour, then put in a blender or food processor with the remaining ingredients and blend until smooth.

4. Spread the salted caramel in a thick layer on top of the dehydrated or frozen crust.

5. Make the banana filling: In the food processor, blend all the ingredients, then pour the filling on top of the caramel layer and place in the freezer for 20 minutes to set up.

6. Meanwhile, whip up your coconut cream: Take the cans of coconut milk out of the fridge, flip them over, open with a can opener, and pour out any liquid. You can save this liquid and add to smoothies. What you really want is the solid part. Add the solid coconut milk to a bowl and whisk by hand or with a hand mixer to create whipped cream.

7. Spread the whipped coconut cream on top of the frozen banana layer and return to the freezer for another 20 minutes to set up. Keep in the freezer until ready to serve.

RAW. VEGAN. NOT GROSS.

LAVENDER CHEESECAKE

mostly raw • 1 cheesecake; 8 to 10 servings

THIS WAS MY all-time-best-selling-people-still-ask-me-about-it item that I sold at the farmers' market. (It probably cost me five times what I sold it for, though. Have I mentioned that I was a terrible businesswoman?) I've been making it regularly ever since.

This isn't the easiest recipe in this book. It has a lot of ingredients and quite a few steps. But it's creamy and decadent and just so good. It's worth it.

Active time: 2 hours
Inactive time: 4 hours or 12 hours

For the crust:

1 cup beets, coarsely chopped

3 cups coconut flour

1 cup almond flour

2 tablespoons nutritional yeast

1 teaspoon sea salt

1 teaspoon grated lemon zest

2 teaspoons dried lavender

⅓ cup maple syrup

⅓ cup coconut oil

For the white layer:

2 cups fresh coconut meat

1 cup raw cashews, soaked in water for at least 1 hour

1 cup agave nectar

¼ cup fresh lemon juice

½ cup coconut oil

Seeds of ½ vanilla bean, scraped out with a spoon

½ teaspoon sea salt

For the pink layer:

2 cups fresh coconut meat

1 cup raw cashews, soaked in water

1 cup agave nectar

¼ cup fresh lemon juice

½ cup coconut oil

½ cup beet juice

½ teaspoon sea salt

2 teaspoons culinary lavender

¼ cup nutritional yeast

1. Make the crust: In a food processor, pulse the beets a few times, then add the remaining crust ingredients and process again, but keep the mixture somewhat chunky.

2. Press the crust into a 9-inch springform, making sure to reinforce the sides so they don't break, and dehydrate overnight or bake in the oven at its lowest temperature for 2 to 3 hours, until crust is firm to touch. Let cool completely.

3. Make the white layer: Put all the ingredients in a blender and blend until smooth.

4. Once the crust has cooled, pour the white layer into it and place in the refrigerator to set up for at least 30 minutes.

5. Make the pink layer: Put all the ingredients in a blender and blend until smooth. Pour over the white layer.

6. Refrigerate or freeze for at least 30 minutes.

7. Keep in the freezer until ready to serve.

BLUEBERRY TART

mostly raw • 1 tart; 8 to 10 servings

THE NICE THING ABOUT this tart is that you can make it year round, and just change the fruit based on what's in season. Summertime? Use berries or stone fruits like peaches. Fall? I love to use persimmons for that bright orange flavor. Spring? Cherries are gorgeous and add the perfect sweet-and-sour balance. Winter? Apples are great—just toss them with a little lemon juice and maple syrup to prevent browning.

Active time: 2 hours
Inactive time: 2 hours or 12 hours

For the crust:

3 cups walnuts

3 tablespoons maple syrup

1 tablespoon coconut oil

½ teaspoon salt

1 tablespoon vanilla extract

1½ teaspoons salt

1 teaspoon cinnamon

½ teaspoon freshly grated nutmeg

For the filling:

3 cups walnuts, soaked in water for at least 5 hours or up to overnight, then drained

¾ cup agave nectar

¾ cup coconut oil

For the fruit topping:

3 cups blueberries

1. Make the crust: Put the walnuts in a food processor and process for about 10 seconds. Add the remaining crust ingredients and process again, but keep the mixture somewhat chunky.

2. Press the crust into a 8-inch tart pan, making sure to reinforce the sides so they don't break, and dehydrate overnight or bake in the oven at its lowest temperature. (Alternatively, place the crust in the freezer for about 1 hour so that it can firm up—just be aware that it'll soften when you bring it back to room temp.)

3. Make the filling: Put the walnuts in the food processor and process until finely ground, then add the agave nectar, coconut oil, and vanilla and pulse to combine. Finally add the salt, cinnamon, and nutmeg and pulse once to combine.

4. Pour the filling into the prepared crust and place in the freezer for 20 to 30 minutes to set up.

5. Top the tart with berries and return to the freezer for at least 20 minutes or until ready to serve.

CHILE TRUFFLES

raw • 12 truffles

REPLY TO THAT "Ladies' Night Dinner Party" e-mail thread that you will be bringing dessert this time, and prepare to receive high accolades from all your chocolate-loving lady friends. These truffles are incredibly decadent, but also pack a fiery punch that rounds out the rich flavor.

One trick is to refrigerate the dough before you try to roll it into balls—it'll keep the dough from sticking to your fingers and save you a lot of frustration. The chocolate coating remains solid as long as you keep your truffles under 78°F (the melting point for coconut oil), so just keep the truffles in the fridge or freezer until you're ready to serve them.

To make mint truffles, omit the chile and cayenne and add 2 teaspoons peppermint extract.

Active time: 30 minutes
Inactive time: 1 hour

For the truffle base:

1 cup shredded coconut

2 cups walnuts

¾ cup cocoa powder

½ cup agave nectar or maple syrup

½ cup coconut oil

1 teaspoon sea salt

1 tablespoon vanilla extract

2 tablespoons ground pasilla chile

2 teaspoons ground cayenne

For the chocolate shell:

1 cup coconut oil

½ cup agave nectar or maple syrup

½ cup cocoa powder

1 teaspoon salt

1 teaspoon vanilla extract

Optional:

Ground cayenne and/or paprika (to indicate HOT!) or sea salt

1. Make the truffle base: In a food processor, combine the coconut and walnuts, and process for 15 to 30 seconds. Add the remaining truffle base ingredients and process until incorporated.

2. Put the base in the refrigerator for 20 minutes to chill.

3. Roll into truffle-size balls (or slightly smaller) and place on a parchment-lined baking sheet. Place in the freezer for 20 to 30 minutes.

4. Make the chocolate shell: Combine all the shell ingredients in a food processor or blender.

5. Remove the truffle balls from the freezer and dip into the chocolate shell with a fork.

6. Set the truffles back on the parchment paper, sprinkle with cayenne, paprika, or sea salt, if desired, and return them to the freezer to set up for at least 30 minutes.

CHOCOLATE AVOCADO PUDDING

raw • 3 or 4 servings

I RECOMMEND MAKING THIS for everyone you love who thinks raw food is gross. Then you get to hit them with the it's-actually-made-out-of-avocados! punch line after they've already tried it. I haven't served this to one person who hasn't loved it. The avocados create an amazingly light, airy, and creamy pudding texture. The tamari and balsamic vinegar might seem like bizarre ingredients for a pudding, but they are actually there to make the chocolate flavor a little more complex. They also knock out any hint of avocado. I swear this doesn't taste like chocolate guacamole at all.

Active time: 15 minutes

2 large avocados, pitted and peeled

½ cup agave nectar or maple syrup

½ cup cocoa powder

3 tablespoons coconut oil

½ teaspoon balsamic vinegar

½ teaspoon tamari

¼ teaspoon salt

1. Blend all the ingredients in a food processor until smooth.

2. Enjoy as is, or freeze in a glass container to enjoy later.

CHIA PUDDING POPS

mostly raw • 6 to 8 popsicles

I WAS OBSESSED WITH POPSICLES when I was little. I remember once being shamed by my sisters when they realized that I had eaten eighteen (Did you hear that? EIGHTEEN) popsicles out of the twenty-one-pack my mom had bought the day before. Have I mentioned that I like popsicles?

One of my favorites was pudding pops, something I've tried to find a vegan version of in grocery stores but to no avail. These chia pops are a far cry from those chemical- and corn syrup–laden ones I used to love. They are sweet and creamy, and are especially decadent when covered in the chocolate shell!

Active time: 15 minutes
Inactive time: 30 minutes

3 cups almond milk

⅓ cup chia seeds

⅓ cup honey or maple syrup

1 teaspoon vanilla extract

Chocolate shell (see page 187)

1. Combine the almond milk, chia seeds, honey, and vanilla in a large measuring cup or spouted bowl and let sit for 30 minutes, continually stirring to make sure you get rid of any clumps.

2. Pour the mixture into popsicle molds.

3. Remove the popsicles from their molds, dip them in the chocolate shell, then place on a waxed paper–lined tray and return to the freezer until ready to serve.

NUTTY BUTTER CUPS

mostly raw • *24 cups*

THE TRICK WITH THESE IS to pour the chocolate mixture into the bottom of each cupcake liner, but then to tilt it around in all directions, letting it thin out and spread up the sides. The tilting ensures that the sides will be covered in chocolate, and it also keeps the base crisp and uniform as far as thickness. You want a perfect chocolate-to-almond butter ratio, after all!

Active time: 10 minutes
Inactive time: 3 hours

½ cup cocoa powder

½ cup maple syrup

⅓ cup coconut oil

½ cup almond butter

1. Blend the cocoa powder, maple syrup, and coconut oil in a blender or food processor until smooth.

2. Pour into the bottom of cupcake liners, tilting to spread the chocolate evenly, and place in the freezer to set up.

3. Remove from the freezer, add 1 teaspoon almond butter to each, then cover with more chocolate mixture.

4. Return the cups to the freezer for at least 1 hour and keep them in the freezer until ready to serve.

RAW. VEGAN. NOT GROSS.

NUTTY BUTTER CUP ICE CREAM

raw • 6 to 8 servings

ONCE I'VE MADE a batch of Nutty Butter Cups, the obvious next step is turn them into ice cream. The cashews and coconut just add to all that nutty goodness.

Active time: 30 minutes
Inactive time: 4 hours

2 cups raw cashews, soaked in water overnight and drained

2 cups fresh coconut meat

1 cup coconut water

¾ cup agave nectar

½ teaspoon salt

Seeds of 1 vanilla bean, scraped out with a spoon, or 2 teaspoons vanilla extract

½ cup coconut oil (liquid)

3 to 4 Nutty Butter Cups (page 192), broken into pieces

1. Put the cashews, coconut meat, coconut water, agave nectar, salt, and vanilla in a blender and blend until smooth.

2. Add the coconut oil (make sure it's in liquid form, not solidified) and blend again.

3. If you have an ice cream maker, use it according to the machine's instructions. If not, place the mixture in a bowl and put it in the freezer for 3 to 4 hours, stirring it every 30 minutes or so.

4. When the ice cream is almost done, fold in small chunks of the almond butter cups.

5. Return to the freezer to let it finish setting up for at least 1 hour.

LAVENDER MACAROONS

mostly raw • 6 servings

I HAVE MADE THOUSANDS OF these lavender macaroons, but I still get such a thrill when I press the button to grind the lavender in my coffee grinder. A soothing spa-like aroma fills the kitchen. The coconut, lavender, and almond blend so beautifully to make perfect little mounds that are crispy on the outside and moist on the inside.

Active time: 30 minutes
Inactive time: 1 hour or 12 hours

3 cups shredded coconut

1 cup almond flour

2 teaspoons culinary lavender, ground extra fine in a coffee grinder

½ teaspoon coarse sea salt

1 cup maple syrup

⅓ cup coconut oil

1 tablespoon vanilla extract

1. In a large bowl, combine the coconut, almond flour, lavender, and salt.

2. In a smaller bowl, combine the maple syrup, coconut oil, and vanilla.

3. Add the wet ingredients to the dry mixture and stir until combined.

4. Take 2 to 3 tablespoons of the mixture, loosely roll into a ball, and place on a teflex sheet or a baking sheet lined with parchment paper.

5. Dehydrate overnight or bake in the oven at 200°F for 1 to 2 hours, until they are crispy on the outside but still moist on the inside.

CHOCOLATE CREAM PIE

mostly raw • 1 pie; 8 to 10 servings

WITH A CRISPY CRUST, creamy coconut base, and intense chocolate layer, this is a charming final course to finish off a red wine–heavy dinner. I love the look of the contrasting layers when you slice into it.

Active time: 2 hours
Inactive time: 3 hours or 12 hours

For the crust:

3 cups raw cashews

1 cup cocoa powder

4 to 5 dates, pitted

2 tablespoons maple syrup

1 tablespoon coconut oil

Pinch of sea salt

For the chocolate layer:

1 cup cocoa powder

1 cup maple syrup

½ cup coconut oil

For the vanilla coconut cream:

2 coconuts

1 cup raw cashews, soaked in water overnight

1 cup coconut oil

1 tablespoon vanilla extract

¼ teaspoon salt

1. Make the crust: Place the cashews in a food processor and process for about 10 seconds. Add the remaining ingredients and process again, but keep the mixture somewhat chunky.

2. Press the mixture into a 8-inch pie tin, making sure to reinforce the sides so they don't break, and dehydrate overnight or bake in the oven at its lowest temperature for 1 to 2 hours. Let cool completely. (Alternatively, place the crust in the freezer for about 1 hour so that it can firm up—just be aware that it'll soften when you bring it back to room temp.)

3. Make the chocolate layer: Combine all the ingredients and pour into the cooled crust. Place in the freezer for at least 30 minutes to set up.

4. Make the vanilla coconut cream: Scrape the coconut meat out of the coconuts and put it in a high-speed blender. Drain and add the cashews, 1/2 cup water, and all the remaining coconut cream ingredients to the blender. Blend until smooth.

5. Pour the coconut cream mixture on top of the chocolate layer and return to the freezer for at least 30 minutes to set up.

6. Keep in the freezer until ready to serve.

ICED BROWNIES

mostly raw • 2 dozen

WHILE YOU MIGHT FIRST BE surprised by how thin these brownies are, as soon as you take one bite you'll understand why. They are incredibly dense, and covered with a chocolate fudge icing. If you're looking to get a serious chocolate fix, this is it.

Active time: 30 minutes
Inactive time: 3 hours or 18 hours

For the brownies:

1 cup almond milk or water

1 cup maple syrup

Seeds from 1 vanilla bean, scraped out with a spoon, or 1½ teaspoons vanilla extract

3 cups cocoa powder

1½ teaspoons salt

4 cups cashew flour

For the chocolate icing:

1 cup coconut oil

3 tablespoons maple syrup

Pinch of sea salt

2 teaspoons cinnamon

1 cup cocoa powder

¼ cup cacao nibs

1. Make the brownies: In a food processor, combine the almond milk, maple syrup, and vanilla and process to combine. Add the cocoa powder and salt and process until well combined.

2. Pour the mixture into a bowl and fold in the cashew flour.

3. Using a spatula, spread the batter about ¹/₂-inch thick onto a teflex-lined dehydrator sheet (or a parchment-paper–lined pan if using an oven) and dehydrate overnight or bake in the oven at 200°F for 1 hour.

4. Flip the brownies using a large spatula, then dehydrate for 5 hours more, or bake in the oven for 1 hour more. Let cool completely.

5. Make the chocolate icing: In a food processor, combine the coconut oil, maple syrup, salt, cinnamon, and cocoa powder and process until smooth.

6. Pour the icing over the brownies, sprinkle with cacao nibs, then place in the refrigerator for 30 minutes to set up.

7. Cut into squares and store in the refrigerator or freezer until ready to serve.

BLACKBERRIES WITH BASIL
AND COCONUT CREAM

mostly raw • *4 servings*

IF YOU'VE GOTTEN YOUR HANDS on some perfectly ripe berries, don't mess with them. Nothing you can do will be able to compete with the plump mouthfeel of fresh blackberries. This really goes for any fruit that's in season: peaches, apricots, cherries—anything that is so beautiful and juicy it makes you want to cry. Just top it with coconut cream, a little balsamic vinegar, and a bit of basil and call it a day. A very, very good day.

Active time: 5 minutes

2 (13.5-ounce) cans full-fat coconut milk (no additives or no guar gum), chilled in the cans overnight

¼ teaspoon maple syrup (optional)

2 to 3 cups fresh blackberries

¼ cup balsamic vinegar

4 or 5 fresh basil leaves, cut into chiffonade

1. Take the cans of coconut milk out of the fridge, flip them over, open with a can opener, and pour out any liquid. You can save this liquid and add to smoothies. What you really want is the solid part. Add the solid coconut milk to a bowl and whisk by hand or with a hand mixer to create whipped cream. Add the maple syrup, if desired.

2. Divide the blackberries among serving bowls and top with a dollop of whipped cream, a drizzle of vinegar, and some basil.

BROWNIE POPSICLES

mostly raw • 6 to 8 popsicles

I LOVE BEING ABLE TO use the crumbs and funny-looking end pieces of the brownies to make a whole new dessert. It reminds me of my childhood favorite "cookies and cream" ice cream popsicles—I love biting into the popsicle and getting a big chunk of brownie.

Active time: 10 minutes
Inactive time: 3 hours

1 (13 to 14-ounce) can full-fat coconut milk

½ cup maple syrup

Pinch of salt

3 to 4 Iced Brownies (page 200)

1. Combine the coconut milk, maple syrup, and salt in a blender and blend for a few seconds.

2. Add the brownies and pulse a few times.

3. Pour into popsicle molds, add sticks, and freeze until solid.

ACKNOWLEDGMENTS

EMILY MRAZ, for handling both panic attacks and logistics, for knowing I need help before I do, and for always bringing cocktails.

ZACH SCHISGAL, for thinking I'm not as dumb as I look, and for putting up with my terrible communication skills.

WILL SCHWALBE and KARA ROTA, for taking a chance on a weirdo with a man voice, and for tolerating me while I tried to figure out how to write a book. Thank you for letting me be myself.

DAVID LOFTUS, for the gorgeous photos, for your gentle way, and for loving my dog so much.

SOPHIA GREEN, for your creative brilliance, for your kitchen prowess, and for hustling so hard for me. You are a force to be reckoned with. I'm so glad I'm on your team.

JAMIE DORE, for being a salt-of-the-earth badass. I am so proud of you.

ERIC SLATKIN, for pushing me to be myself in front of a camera, and for thinking at least some of my jokes are funny.

TASTEMADE, for giving me the opportunity to spread the vegan message in my own weird way.

NAMI KURITA, for making this book more beautiful than I'd ever imagined.

DIANE PEREZ, for sharing your passion to create a healthier future for the next generation.

RAMY ROMANY, SHARRA ROMANY, CHRIS LOWE, JUSTIN GAY, CARLO ALBERTO ORECCHIA, and LINDA SAMMUT, for helping me feel like an actual human in front of a camera and for becoming my real-life friends.

ALEX HEALY and NOAH SANDERS, for taking me in when I needed it most. Sidesaddle and Old Hat were destined to be friends.

SAM CONKLING, for helping me build Sidesaddle Kitchen and teaching me to be creative.

MARILEE STARK, for giving me a voice and for keeping me alive.

MECHELE AND KATIE, for supporting me and making fun of me when I need it most.

ELENA, for being the middle-of-the-day phone call that I can always make.

ERIC, for opening up my brain and heart. Finding you has changed everything.

BUZZ, for sitting at my feet, from the first words typed to the last.

WEAR WHAT YOU EAT

#FROOBS HOW-TO:

1. Pick any seasonal fruit.

2. If fruit is especially large, cut in half.

3. Hold one on each side of chest area.

4. Remember that big, small, lopsided, warped, damaged—all froobs are beautiful.

FRUITY NECKLACE HOW-TO:

1. Pick a fruit that's not too delicate, but not too hard to puncture.

2. Grab clear fishing line and a tapestry needle.

3. Thread one by one until you've got a desired length.

4. Tie around your neck.

5. Go out in public and brace yourself for compliments.

VEGGIE WIG HOW-TO:

1. For minimal pain, pick a veg that's lightweight (i.e. kale, spinach, chives). It really depends on how voluminous you want your hair to be. Me? I like a lot of volume, so I know that means I've gotta put up with a decent amount of plant weight on my head. Plant weight on head = pain.

2. Find a wreath frame that fits well and can sit on top of your head without you holding on to it.

3. Take each individual leaf/fruit/herb and attach to the wreath with floral wire, going around ¾ of the way, but leaving ¼ of the frame open—that's where your face will be!

4. Continue until your hands are bleeding and you can't remember why you're doing this anymore.

5. Put on your veggie wig and hit the clubs.

INDEX

www.flatironbooks.com

The Library of Congress Cataloging-in-Publication Data is available upon request.

ISBN 978-1-250-06690-9 (hardcover)
ISBN 978-1-250-06691-6 (e-book)

Our books may be purchased in bulk for promotional, educational, or business use. Please contact your local bookseller or Macmillan Corporate and Premium Sales Department at 1-800-221-7945 x 5442 or by email at MacmillanSpecialMarkets@macmillan.com.

First Edition: May 2016

10 9 8 7 6 5 4 3 2 1